IAMBLICHUS OF CHALCIS:
THE LETTERS

Society of Biblical Literature

Writings from the Greco-Roman World

David Konstan and Johan C. Thom, General Editors

Editorial Board

David Armstrong
Elizabeth Asmis
Brian E. Daley, S.J.
David G. Hunter
Wendy Mayer
Margaret M. Mitchell
Ilaria Ramelli
Michael J. Roberts
James C. VanderKam

Number 19

Iamblichus of Chalcis:
The Letters

Volume Editor: Johan C. Thom

IAMBLICHUS OF CHALCIS:
THE LETTERS

Edited with a Translation and Commentary by

John M. Dillon

and

Wolfgang Polleichtner

Society of Biblical Literature
Atlanta

IAMBLICHUS OF CHALCIS:
THE LETTERS

Copyright © 2009 by the Society of Biblical Literature

All rights reserved. No part of this work may be reproduced or transmitted in any form or by any means, electronic or mechanical, including photocopying and recording, or by means of any information storage or retrieval system, except as may be expressly permitted by the 1976 Copyright Act or in writing from the publisher. Requests for permission should be addressed in writing to the Rights and Permissions Office, Society of Biblical Literature, 825 Houston Mill Road, Atlanta, GA 30329 USA.

Library of Congress Cataloging-in-Publication Data

Iamblichus, ca. 250-ca. 330.
   [Correspondence. English and Greek. 2009]
   Iamblichus of Chalcis : the letters / edited with a translation and commentary by John M. Dillon and Wolfgang Polleichtner.
      p. cm. — (Writings from the Greco-Roman world ; no. 19)
   Includes bibliographical references and indexes.
   ISBN: 978-1-58983-161-2 (pbk. : alk. paper)
   1. Iamblichus, ca. 250-ca. 330—Correspondence. 2. Iamblichus, ca. 250–ca. 330. I. Dillon, John M. II. Polleichtner, Wolfgang. III. Title.
   B669.Z7A4 2009
   186'.4 —dc22   2009028007

17 16 15 14 13 12 11 10 09   5 4 3 2 1
Printed in the United States of America on acid-free, recycled paper
conforming to ANSI/NISO Z39.48-1992 (R1997) and ISO 9706:1994
standards for paper permanence.

Contents

Preface vii
Abbreviations ix

Introduction xiii
   1. Life and Works xiii
   2. Philosophical Epistolography xv
   3. Iamblichus's Correspondents xvii
   4. The Philosophy of the Letters xix
   5. Characteristics of Style and Vocabulary xxii
   6. A Note on the Text xxiv

Text and Translation
   Letter 1: To Agrippa, On Ruling 2
   Letter 2: To Anatolius, On Justice 4
   Letter 3: To Arete, On Self-Control 6
   Letter 4: To Asphalius, On Wisdom 12
   Letter 5: To Dexippus, On Dialectic 14
   Letter 6: To Dyscolius, On Ruling (?) 16
   Letter 7: To Eustathius, On Music 18
   Letter 8: To Macedonius, On Fate 20
   Letter 9: To Macedonius, On Concord 28
   Letter 10: To Olympius, On Courage 30
   Letter 11: To Poemenius, On Providence (?) 32
   Letter 12: To Sopater, On Fate 34
   Letter 13: To Sopater, On Dialectic 36
   Letter 14: To Sopater, On Bringing Up Children 40
   Letter 15: To Sopater, On Ingratitude 44
   Letter 16: To Sopater, On Virtue 46
   Letter 17: To Sopater, On Self-Respect 50
   Letter 18: To Sopater, On Truth 50
   Letter 19: To an Unknown Recipient, On Marriage 52
   Letter 20: To an Unknown Recipient, On Ruling (?) 52

Testimonium 1: To an Unknown Recipient,
  On the Descent of Souls (?) 54
Textimonium 2 54

Commentary
  Letter 1: To Agrippa, On Ruling 59
  Letter 2: To Anatolius, On Justice 61
  Letter 3: To Arete, On Self-Control 62
  Letter 4: To Asphalius, On Wisdom 67
  Letter 5: To Dexippus, On Dialectic 68
  Letter 6: To Dyscolius, On Ruling (?) 70
  Letter 7: To Eustathius, On Music 72
  Letter 8: To Macedonius, On Fate 73
  Letter 9: To Macedonius, On Concord 78
  Letter 10: To Olympius, On Courage 80
  Letter 11: To Poemenius, On Providence (?) 82
  Letter 12: To Sopater, On Fate 83
  Letter 13: To Sopater, On Dialectic 83
  Letter 14: To Sopater, On Bringing Up Children 85
  Letter 15: To Sopater, On Ingratitude 86
  Letter 16: To Sopater, On Virtue 87
  Letter 17: To Sopater, On Self-Respect 89
  Letter 18: To Sopater, On Truth 90
  Letter 19: To an Unknown Recipient, On Marriage 91
  Letter 20: To an Unknown Recipient, On Ruling (?) 93
  Testimonium 1: To an Unknown Recipient,
    On the Descent of Souls (?) 94
  Textimonium 2 96

Bibliography 99
Index rerum 101
Index verborum 111

Preface

This edition is the result of a very pleasant and fruitful collaboration. It arose in the following way. Many years ago, JD (John Dillon) made a collection, with translation, of the fragments of the *Letters* of Iamblichus preserved by John of Stobi in his *Anthologium* but did nothing further with them, being somewhat uncertain whether they really merited publishing, and if they did, what sort of commentary would be appropriate to them. They are, after all, as we note in the introduction, "popular philosophy" and, as such, give very few hints, if any, of the complexities of Iamblichus's "serious" philosophical position.

They rested, therefore, in a notebook for about a quarter of a century, until, in the later 1990s, JD received an enquiry from his friend Michael Erler, of Würzburg, saying that a student of his, WP (Wolfgang Polleichtner), had it in mind to edit the *Letters* for a doctoral thesis, if they were not already being dealt with by JD. JD replied that there was this notebook, but if WP wished to proceed with an edition of his own, he could go ahead. At the same time, Michael Erler and WP received word that there was another project on the *Letters* already well underway in Italy. That understandably proved rather discouraging.

Early in 2004, however, WP happened to call into Trinity College Dublin in order to spend the Hilary term of that year studying with Damien Nelis during his preparation of his dissertation and introduced himself, whereupon JD proposed that he might like to join in an edition after all, as nothing more had yet been done. And so came about this collaboration, conducted at a distance, WP being initially in Austin, Texas, and subsequently in Bochum, JD remaining in Dublin, but constantly in touch electronically. WP has reedited the text[1] and collaborated in the

---

1. We have based ourselves on the text of Curt Wachsmuth and Otto Hense, eds., *Ioannis Stobaei anthologium* (5 vols. in 4; Berlin: Weidmann, 1884–1923; repr., Berlin: Weidmann, 1958), since a previous study of one of two surviving manuscripts (the Parisinus, fifteenth century), in connection with an edition of Iamblichus's *De Anima* (John F.

composition of the notes and introduction. Iamblichus's text was translated into English by JD. We have come in the process to appreciate the *Letters* for what they are: something like a series of philosophical "calling cards," of a type not otherwise attested in the Platonist tradition, addressed to both Iamblichus's own students (and even his old teacher), as well as to a selection of (we assume) prominent figures in the society of late antique Syria (and perhaps further afield) and in the Imperial administration. As such, they give us a welcome insight both into the popular, nonspecialist philosophical discourse of the Neoplatonic period and into Iamblichus's role as a public figure, as attested otherwise chiefly by his biographer Eunapius of Sardis.

We are most grateful to John Fitzgerald, David Konstan, and Johan Thom, representing the Society of Biblical Literature's Writings from the Greco-Roman World series, for being prepared to take on this project and to guide it to a conclusion. We are indebted also to Adrien Lecerf, Ecole Normale Superieure, Paris, for drawing our attention to the reference to the *Letters* in Olympiodorus (*Testimonium* 2).

John M. Dillon
Wolfgang Polleichtner

Finamore and John M. Dillon, *Iamblichus' De Anima: Text, Translation, and Commentary* [Philosophia antiqua 92. Leiden: Brill, 2002]) assured JD of the basic reliability of Wachsmuth and Hense's text.

Abbreviations

Primary Sources

Abst.	Porphyry, *De abstinentia* (*On Abstinence*)
Alc.	Plato, *Alcibiades*
An.	Iamblichus, *De anima* (*On the Soul*)
An. procr.	Plutarch, *De animae procreatione in Timaeo*
Anth.	Stobaeus, *Anthologium* (*Anthology*)
Apol.	Lucian, *Apologia* (*Apology*)
Aristides	Aristides, *Orationes* (*Orations*)
C. Ap.	Josephus, *Contra Apionem* (*Against Apion*)
Cael. hier.	Dionysius the Areopagite, *De caelesti hierarchia*
Comm. math.	Iamblichus, *De communi mathematica scientia*
Crat.	Plato, *Cratylus*
Cur. acut.	Aretaeus, *Cura acutorum morborum* (*On the Cure of Acute Diseases*)
Cyr.	Xenophon, *Cyropaedia* (*Education of Cyrus*)
Def.	Plato, *Definitiones* (*Definitions*)
Demosthenes	Demosthenes, *Orationes* (*Orations*)
Did.	Alcinous, *Didaskalikos* (*Handbook of Platonism*)
Diogenes Laertius	Diogenes Laertius, *Vitae philosophorum*
Dogm. Plat.	Apuleius, *De dogmate Platonis*
Enn.	Plotinus, *Enneads*
Ep.	*Epistulae* (*Letters*)
Eth. eud.	Aristotle, *Ethica eudemia* (*Eudemian Ethics*)
Eth. nic.	Aristotle, *Ethica nichomachea* (*Nichomachean Ethics*)
Gen. corr.	Aristotle, *De generatione et corruptione* (*Generation and Corruption*)
Gorg.	Plato, *Gorgias*
Hal.	Oppian, *Halieutica*
Hel.	Gorgias, *Helena* (*Encomium of Helen*)
Herodotus	Herodotus, *Historiae* (*Histories*)

Hipp. maj.	Plato, *Hippias major* (*Greater Hippias*)
Hipp. min.	Plato, *Hippias minor* (*Lesser Hippias*)
Hist.	Dio Cassius, *Historiae Romanae* (*Roman History*)
Hist. an.	Aristotle, *Historia animalium* (*History of Animals*)
Id.	Theocritus, *Idylls*
In Gorg.	Olympiodorus, *In Platonis Gorgiam commentaria* (*Commentary on Plato's* Gorgias)
In Met.	Syrianus, *In Aristotelis Metaphysica commentaria* (*Commentary on Aristotle's* Metaphysics)
In Nic.	Iamblichus, *In Nicomachi arithmeticam introductionem*
In Parm.	Iamblichus, *In Parmenidem* (*Commentary on the* Parmenides)
In Phaed.	Damascius, *In Platonis Phaedonem commentaria* (*Commentary on Plato's* Phaedo)
In Soph.	Iamblichus, *In Sophistam* (*Commentary on the* Sophist)
In Tim.	Calcidius, *Commentarius in Platonis Timaeum* (*Commentary on Plato's* Timaeus); Iamblichus, *In Timaeum* (*Commentary on the* Timaeus)
In. Top.	Alexander Aphrodisiensis, *In Aristotelis Topicorum libros octo commentaria*
Leg.	Plato, *Leges* (*Laws*)
Mem.	Xenophon, *Memorabilia*
Metaph.	Aristotle, *Metaphysica* (*Metaphysics*)
Mor.	Plutarch, *Moralia*
Mos.	Philo, *De vita Mosis* (*On the Life of Moses*)
Mund.	Pseudo-Aristotle, *De mundo* (*On the Universe*)
Myst.	Iamblichus, *De mysteriis* (*On the Mysteries*)
Od.	Homer, *Odyssea* (*Odyssey*)
Omn. doctr.	Michael Psellus, *De omnifaria doctrina*
Or.	*Orationes* (*Orations*)
Orest.	Euripides, *Orestes*
Phd.	Plato, *Phaedo*
Phdr.	Plato, *Phaedrus*
Phileb.	Plato, *Philebus*
Phys.	Aristotle, *Physica* (*Physics*)
Pol.	Aristotle, *Politica* (*Politics*)
Prob.	[Aristotle], *Problemata* (*Problems*)
Prop. an.	Galen, *De propriorum animi cuiuslibet affectuum dignotione et curatione*

Prot.	Plato, *Protagoras*
Protr.	Iamblichus, *Protrepticus*
Pseudol.	Lucian, *Pseudologista* (*The Mistaken Critic*)
Pyth. orac.	Plutarch, *De Pythiae oraculis*
Resp.	Plato, *Respublica* (*Republic*)
Rhet.	Aristotle, *Rhetorica* (*Rhetoric*)
Schol. Thuc.	*Scholia in Thucydidem*. See Hude below.
Sent.	Porphyry, *Sententiae ad intelligibilia ducentes*
Soph.	Plato, *Sophista* (*Sophist*)
Strom.	Clement of Alexandria, *Stromata* (*Miscellanies*)
Symp.	Plato, *Symposium*
Theaet.	Plato, *Theaetetus*
Them.	Plutarch, *Themistocles*
Tim.	Plato, *Timaeus*
Vit. Apoll.	Philostratus, *Vita Apollonii*
Vit. phil.	Eunapius, *Vitae philosophorum et sophistarum* (*Lives of the Philosophers and Sophists*); Diogenes Laertius, *Vitae philosophorum* (*Lives of the Philosophers*)
Vit. Pyth.	Iamblichus, *De Vita Pythagorica* (*On the Pythagorean Way of Life*)

Secondary Sources

BT	Bibliotheca scriptorum Graecorum et Romanorum Teubneriana
LCL	Loeb Classical Library
PLRE	Jones, Arnold H. M., John R. Martindale, and J. Morris. *The Prosopography of the Later Roman Empire*. 3 vols. Cambridge: Cambridge University Press, 1971–1992.
SBLTT	Society of Biblical Literature Texts and Translations
SVF	*Stoicorum veterum fragmenta*. Edited by Hans Friedrich August von Arnim. 4 vols. Leipzig: Teubner, 1903–1924.

Short References

Bergk = Bergk, Theodor, ed. *Poetae lyrici graeci*. 4th ed. 3 vols. Leipzig: Teubner, 1878–1882.

Diels-Kranz = Diels, Hermann, and Walther Kranz, eds. *Die Fragmente* der Vorsokratiker: Griechisch und Deutsch. 7th ed. 3 vols. Berlin: Weidmann, 1954.

Dillon = Dillon, John M., ed. and trans. *Iamblichi Chalcidensis in Platonis dialogos commentariorum fragmenta*. Philosophia antiqua 23. Leiden: Brill, 1973.

Festa = Festa, Nicola, ed. *De communi mathematica scientia liber: Ad fidem codicis Florentini*. Leipzig: Teubner, 1891.

Finamore-Dillon = Finamore, John F., and John M. Dillon. *Iamblichus' De Anima: Text, Translation, and Commentary*. Philosophia antiqua 92. Leiden: Brill, 2002.

Gallop = Gallop, David, trans. *Plato: Phaedo*. Oxford: Clarendon, 1975.

Heil-Ritter = Heil, Günter, and Adolf Martin Ritter, eds. *Corpus Dionysiacum 2: De coelesti hierarchia, De ecclesiastica hierarchia, De mystica theologia, Epistulae*. Patristische Texte und Studien 36. Berlin: de Gruyter, 1991.

Hense = See Wachsmuth-Hense below.

Hude = Hude, Karl, ed. *Scholia in Thucydidem ad optimos codices collata*. Leipzig: Teubner, 1927. Repr., New York: Arno, 1973.

Kock = Kock, Theodor. *Comicorum Atticorum fragmenta*. Vol. 2. Leipzig: Teubner, 1884.

Kroll = Kroll, Wilhelm, ed. *Syriani in metaphysica commentaria*. Commentaria in Aristotelem Graeca 6.1. Berlin: Reimer, 1902.

Mullach = Mullach, Friedrich Wilhelm August, ed. *Fragmenta philosophorum graecorum*. Scriptorum graecorum bibliotheca. 3 vols. Paris: Didot, 1867–1881.

Norvin = Norvin, William, ed. *Olympiodori philosophi In Platonis Phaedonem commentaria*. BSGRT. Leipzig: Teubner, 1913. Repr., Hildesheim: Olms, 1968.

Pistelli = Pistelli, Ermenegildo. *Protrepticus: Ad fidem codicis florentini*. BSGRT. Leipzig: Teubner, 1888.

Saunders = Saunders, Trevor J., trans. *Plato: The Laws*. Harmondsworth, Eng.: Penguin, 1970.

Smith = Smith, Andrew, ed. *Porphyrii philosophi fragmenta*. BSGRT. Stuttgart: Teubner, 1993.

Thesleff = Thesleff, Holger. *The Pythagorean Texts of the Hellenistic Period*. Åbo: Åbo Akademi, 1965.

Wachsmuth = See Wachsmuth-Hense below.

Wachsmuth-Hense = Wachsmuth, Curt, and Otto Hense, eds. *Ioannis Stobaei anthologium*. 5 vols. in 4. Berlin: Weidmann, 1884–1923. Repr., Berlin: Weidmann, 1958.

Introduction

1. Life and Works

The sources available for our knowledge of Iamblichus's life are highly unsatisfactory, consisting as they do primarily of a hagiographical and ill-informed *Life* by the sophist Eunapius, who was a pupil of Chrysanthius, who was himself a pupil of Iamblichus's pupil Aedesius; nevertheless, enough evidence can be gathered to give a general view of his life span and activities.

The evidence points to a date of birth around 245, in the town of Chalcis-ad-Belum, modern Qinnesrin, in northern Syria. Iamblichus's family were prominent in the area, and the retention of an old Aramaic name (*yamliku*-[*El*]) in the family points to some relationship with the dynasts of Emesa in the previous centuries, one of whose family names this was. This noble ancestry does seem to color somewhat Iamblichus's attitude to tradition—he likes to appeal on occasion for authority to "the most ancient of the priests" (e.g., *An.* 37), and was plainly a recognized authority on Syrian divinities (see Julian, *Hymn to King Helios* 150CD).

As teachers, Eunapius provides (*Vit. phil.* 457–458) two names: first, a certain Anatolius, described as "second in command" to the distinguished Neoplatonic philosopher Porphyry, the pupil of Plotinus; and then Porphyry himself. We are left quite uncertain as to where these contacts took place, but we may presume in Rome, at some time in the 270s or 280s, when Porphyry, on his return from Sicily, had reconstituted Plotinus's school (whatever that involved). If that is so—and it is plain that Iamblichus knew Porphyry's work well, even though he was far from a faithful follower—then it seems probable that he left Porphyry's circle long before the latter's death and returned to his native Syria (probably in the 290s) to set up his own school, not in his hometown, but rather in the city of Apamea, already famous in philosophical circles as the home of the second-century Pythagorizing Platonist Numenius. There he presided over a circle of pupils, including a local grandee, Sopater, who seems to have supported him materially, and as long as Licinius ruled in the East, the school flourished. After the triumph of Constantine, however, the writing had to be on the wall for such an overtly Hellenic and theurgically inclined group, and on Iamblichus's death in the early 320s the school broke up, his senior pupil Aedesius moving to Pergamum, where the Iamblichean tradition was carried on quietly for another generation or so. The emperor Julian, we may note, sought to take on Aedesius as his mentor, but Aedesius, preferring the quiet life, prudently directed him to his own pupil Maximus of Ephesus.

Iamblichus was a prolific author, though unfortunately only his more elementary works survive intact—apart from the *Reply to the Letter of Porphyry to Anebo* (popularly known, since the Renaissance, as *On the Mysteries of the Egyptians*). Chief among these was a sequence of nine, or possibly ten, works in which he presented a comprehensive introduction to Pythagorean philosophy—an indication of his view of Pythagoras as the spiritual grandfather of Platonism. Of these, we still have the first four, beginning with a *Bios Pythagorikos*—not simply a "life of Pythagoras" but rather an account of the Pythagorean way of life, with a biography of Pythagoras woven into it—and followed by an *Exhortation to Philosophy* (*Protreptikos*), a treatise *On the General Science of Mathematics*, and a commentary on the *Introduction to Arithmetic* of the second-century Platonist Nicomachus of Gerasa. The doxographical portion of a treatise *On the Soul*, and extracts from a series of philosophical letters, which are the subject of the present volume, survive in the *Anthologium* of John of Stobi.

Other than those, however, we have considerable evidence of commentaries on works of both Plato and Aristotle, fragments of which survive (mainly) in the later commentaries of Proclus. We have evidence of commentaries on the *Alcibiades*, *Phaedo*, *Phaedrus*, *Sophist*, *Philebus*, *Timaeus*, and *Parmenides* of Plato and the *Categories* of Aristotle (this latter preserved extensively by Simplicius), as well as the *De interpretatione*, *Prior Analytics*, *De caelo*, and *De anima*. He is also on record as having composed a copious commentary on the *Chaldaean Oracles* and a *Platonic Theology*, as well as treatises *On the Gods* and *On the Virtues*. The *Reply to the Letter of Porphyry to Anebo* mentioned above is an odd production, consisting of a response to a polemical open letter by Porphyry attacking the practice and theory of theurgy, which Iamblichus, taking on the persona of a senior Egyptian priest, Abammon, elects to defend.

2. Philosophical Epistolography

Protreptic epistolography as a philosophic genre goes back, so far as we can see, no further than Epicurus, who communicated a significant part of his philosophy in this form. It does not seem to form any part of the Platonist tradition.[1] For Iamblichus, however, we must recognize that the practice of writing philosophic letters went back to the oldest generations of Pythagoreans, even to Pythagoras himself. We do indeed have testimonies, and even fragments, of letters[2] from Pythagoras (to Anaximenes and to King Hiero of Syracuse), as well as from his wife Theano (to eight different correspondents, seven of them female), his daughter Myia (to her friend Phyllis), and his son Telauges (rather anachronistically, to Philolaus).[3] Apart from Pythagoras and his immediate family, we have evidence of letters from Lysis to Hipparchus, from Archytas to Plato (and a reply to this, in the form of Plato's *Ep.* 12), and from the lady Melissa to her friend Cleareta. The fact that all these documents appear to us palpably and woefully bogus is not much to the point; Iamblichus will have accepted them, along with all the other Pythagorean pseudepigrapha, as genuine—as, of course, he would those of Plato. The composition of protreptic epistles, therefore, was for him an activity endowed with the best possible pedigree.[4]

---

1. Those letters of Plato that may possibly be genuine, notably *Ep.* 7 and 8, are really primarily apologiae for his actions (despite the "philosophical digression" in 7) and so do not strictly count as philosophical epistles. The more "philosophical" members of the collection, such as *Ep.* 2 and 6, are of much later provenance—though this was, of course, not obvious to ancient readers. In any case, all of the Platonic epistles are presented as "real" letters rather than epistolary philosophical essays. On Plato's letters, see Michael Erler, *Platon* (Die Philosophie der Antike 2/2; Grundriss der Geschichte der Philosophie; Basel: Schwabe, 2007), 308–22.

2. Most conveniently collected in Holger Thesleff, *The Pythagorean Texts of the Hellenistic Period* (Åbo: Åbo Akademi, 1965).

3. As regards anachronisms, we may note that Theano, in her letter to her friend Rhodope (Thesleff, *Pythagorean Texts*, 200), excuses herself for not sending a copy of "the book of Plato, which is entitled *Ideas*, or *Parmenides*"! It is not easy to penetrate the mental state of the author of such a document.

4. There is evidence of letters also by Aristotle, Theophrastus, and later Peripatetics such as Strato, but these would be of less importance for Iamblichus. We also have, preserved in one manuscript (Cod. Vat. gr. 64), a collection

It is undeniable, however, that there is very little evidence of such epistolography by later Platonists before him. Among the heads of the New Academy, Carneades is attested as having composed letters—and nothing else! (Diogenes Laertius, *Vit. phil.* 4.65)—but they would hardly figure in Iamblichus's pantheon of suitable models. In the vast and varied oeuvre of Plutarch, no epistles are preserved,[5] and from the Neopythagoreans of the second century C.E., Nicomachus of Gerasa and Numenius of Apamea, whom Iamblichus certainly did hold in high honor, there is no sign of a letter surviving (though they may have written them). Only in the case of the Pythagorean "holy man" Apollonius of Tyana (late first century C.E.) do we find a collection of letters—like everything else about that remarkable figure, probably spurious, but good enough for Iamblichus, who would have held him in high regard.

Philosophical epistolography, indeed, in the period of the early Empire, is very much the preserve of Stoics such as Seneca, but he is not someone of whom Iamblichus would have had any knowledge. In the generation or so after Iamblichus, we have an outpouring of letter-writing, philosophical and other, from the pens of such figures as the emperor Julian, the distinguished Antiochene rhetorician Libanius, and the Christian bishop Basil of Caesarea, but prior to Iamblichus, in the late third century C.E., there is precious little evidence of philosophical epistology surviving, and this makes the letters of Iamblichus all the more significant. It is of interest in this connection that two members of Iamblichus's immediate circle are also known as letter-writers: his mysterious admirer (presumably a former student) in Licinius's court whose letters to him became included in the letters of Julian; and the son of his chief pupil Sopater, also called Sopater, of whom a letter (to his brother Himerius) is also preserved by Stobaeus.

---

of letters of "Socrates and the Socratics," including such stalwarts of the Old Academy as Speusippus and Xenocrates—certainly spurious (except perhaps for the *Letter of Speusippus to Philip*—but that is not properly a philosophical epistle) but not without entertainment value—which Iamblichus would presumably have accepted as genuine, if he were acquainted with them.

5. Unless his *Consolations* (παραμυθητικοὶ λόγοι), to his wife, and to a certain Asclepiades (lost; no. 111 in the Lamprias catalogue) should count as letters. There is also record of a "letter" to Favorinus, *On Friendship,* of which a number of fragments are preserved in Stobaeus (frg. 159–71, Francis H. Sandbach, trans., *Fragments* [vol. 15 of *Plutarch's Moralia;* LCL; Cambridge: Harvard University Press, 1969]).

What is it, then, that makes a letter count as a *philosophic* letter?[6] The philosophic letter, as a genre, is really a short philosophical (usually moral) essay, given a lively and personalized slant by being addressed to a particular recipient, usually a friend or student of the author, but sometimes a patron or other public figure. The subject matter of the epistle should doubtless be tailored to some extent to the position or role in life of the recipient (e.g., letters on ruling we might expect to be addressed to senior imperial administrators, or at least local grandees; letters on dialectic to other practicing philosophers), but this need not necessarily be so, if the letter concerns a very general moral topic, such as justice or self-control.

A salient feature of these letters, and one that renders them of great interest for this period, is that they are pitched firmly at the level of popular philosophy. From a perusal of the present collection, one would derive no hint of the complexities of Iamblichus's metaphysical system, nor yet, in the sphere of ethics, of his theory of multiple levels of virtue. Hints of the one can be glimpsed, perhaps, by one who knows, behind his utterances on Providence in the *Letter to Macedonius* and of the other as lurking behind the *Letter to Sopater, On Virtue*; however, in neither case are we presented with any characteristic technicalities. This is philosophy for the general (educated) public, and it reminds us forcefully of the public role in society that all philosophers of this period played, despite their strongly otherworldly tone.[7]

3. Iamblichus's Correspondents

It is a source of considerable frustration to us that we cannot securely identify the great majority of Iamblichus's correspondents in this collection, since we must reckon with the strong probability that most of them

---

6. Even the letters of Seneca to Lucilius do not quite qualify, perhaps, as they come across rather as real letters, combining personal details with philosophic exhortation. It must be admitted, though, that, since what we have of Iamblichus's letters are merely extracts preserved by Stobaeus, there may in fact have been personal details included in the full versions, at the beginning or end.

7. One might reflect that it may be no accident that the nearest analogy to what Iamblichus is doing is to be found in the pastoral epistles of a succession of Christian bishops from Saint Paul on down, except that the bishops are generally addressing their flocks, while Iamblichus is addressing individual recipients, and elite ones at that!

belonged to the higher ranks either of the imperial administration or of Syrian (and perhaps more generally Anatolian) society.

A number of letters, admittedly, are addressed to his pupils: to Dexippus, author of a surviving short introduction to Aristotle's *Categories*, in question and answer form, very appropriately, one on dialectic; to Eustathius, who succeeded to the headship of the School (and moved it to Caesarea in Cappadocia), one on music; and, last but not least, to his favorite pupil (and perhaps also patron) Sopater, a string of letters *On Fate, On Dialectic, On Bringing Up Children* (Sopater being a family man, father of at least two sons, Sopater and Himerius, both of whom went on to distinguished careers in public life), *On Ingratitude, On Virtue, On Self-Respect*. There is also the probability that the Anatolius to whom is addressed a letter *On Justice* is none other than his old teacher, the "second-in-command" to Porphyry.

Beyond these, however, there are pretty slim pickings for the prosopographer. Two, we feel, can be identified with fair certainty: Dyscolius, the recipient of a letter *On Ruling*, bears the same name as a governor of Syria attested for the period around 320 C.E., and this topic would suit him very well; and the lady Arete, recipient of a letter *On Self-Control* (σωφροσύνη), turns up later in the correspondence of the emperor Julian (*Letter to Themistius* 259D), being annoyed by her neighbors in Phrygia, in some unspecified manner—an annoyance from which Julian saved her by appearing in person![8]

Of the others, Agrippa and Macedonius are probably members of the imperial administration and/or the local aristocracy, but no suitable names turn up in the inscriptional material. On the other hand, in the correspondence of Libanius (e.g., *Ep.* 1353) we find a Macedonius listed as the father of certain of his pupils. This man was an advocate who had studied rhetoric under the distinguished sophist Ulpianus and who, on reaching retirement, was appointed *defensor* of Tarsus. Chronologically and geographically, he makes a rather good fit with Iamblichus's cor-

---

8. We cannot, after all, be quite certain that this is the same Arete, but the fact that Julian is prepared to take such trouble on her behalf and refers to her as "that marvelous woman" (ἡ θαυμασία) should indicate her status in Neoplatonist circles. The dating of this intervention is uncertain, but it probably took place in the early 350s, when Arete would necessarily be quite an old woman. Whether she had always been in Phrygia is not clear either; it might be that she decamped from Syria in the wake of Aedesius, when the School was moved to Pergamum.

respondent. Another Macedonius, possible a son or grandson of this man, is mentioned by Libanius as a former pupil and as a φιλόσοφος, as well as an orator (*Ep.* 672–674). We also know of an Olympius who was the father of a pupil of Libanius in the 360s, and this pupil went on to become a doctor in Antioch and was also skilled in grammar and philosophy (*Ep.* 539).

Of Asphalius and Poemenius there is no other trace. However, if we can accord some probability to the identities of Macedonius and Olympius, there begins to emerge a pattern of connections between an earlier generation of Syrian intellectuals, flourishing in the first twenty years of the fourth century, who are acquaintances of Iamblichus in and around Apamea, and a later generation, being educated by, and consorting with, Libanius in Antioch in the middle of the century; we can at least say that there would be nothing strange or unexpected about this.

4. The Philosophy of the Letters

In the surviving fragments, Iamblichus touches on many aspects of philosophy, logical, ethical, and even metaphysical, though not, as we have said above, in such a way as to reveal the more technical levels of his philosophy. However, a distinct philosophical stance is presented here, of which we may summarize the salient aspects.

To take logic first, we find two letters in praise of dialectic: one to Dexippus and one to Sopater. That to Dexippus, as we shall see below, is a rather high-flown production, while that to Sopater is much more prosaic, but both manage to mention the main subjects of logical study, ambiguity, homonymy, induction, elenchus (or refutation), and syllogistic. Above all, the foundational role of dialectic in all philosophical activity is stressed in both epistles.

Ethics is, naturally enough, the chief theme of such documents as these letters. There are praises of Virtue itself as a whole, and all of the four canonical virtues: justice (δικαιοσύνη); self-control (σωφροσύνη); wisdom, or prudence (φρόνησις); and courage (ἀνδρεία). Particularly with respect to this last, but in general with all of them, Iamblichus is disposed to stress the "higher" or "purificatory" aspects of the virtue concerned, though not to the exclusion of its more practical, "civic" applications.[9] The letter to Anatolius, indeed, dwells (in frg. 2) on the

---

9. The categories refer to the distinction made by Plotinus in *Enn.* 1.2

civic aspects of justice, the due apportionment of honors and rewards, leading to civic harmony and goodwill (though it may well have gone on, in what is lost to us, to praise its "higher" aspects as well). That to Arete, on the other hand, stresses rather the capacity of σωφροσύνη to free us from "the pleasures that nail us to the body" and assimilate us to the gods. Φρόνησις, likewise, in the letter to Asphalius, "contemplates the Intellect itself and derives its perfection from it," though it also "has the characteristic of directing men and administering the whole structure of their relations with one another"—though even that "renders those who possess it godlike [θεοειδεῖς]." As for courage, in the letter to Olympius it is presented as "an unshakable intellectual potency and the highest form of intellectual activity, constituting self-identity [ταυτότης] and a state of mind steadfast within itself." Lastly, we have a letter to Sopater on Virtue as a whole, which also stresses its other-worldly aspect. It is "the perfection and proper balance of the life of the soul, the highest and purest activity of reason and intellect and discursive intelligence [διανόησις]," which is characterized by "beauty, symmetry and truth, unchanging identity and simplicity, a transcendent superiority to all other things, and a purity that is raised above all other things and unmixed with them."

Behind all this there is a Neoplatonic theory of grades of virtue, to which Iamblichus himself, in a treatise *On the Virtues* (now lost), had added his own refinements (an ascending scale of fully seven grades, building on the Porphyrian four, as set out in *Sent.* 32), but it remains here, quite properly, very much in the background.

Apart from essays on Virtue and each of the virtues, we have discourses on more properly political topics, such as ruling (to Agrippa and to Dyscolius) and concord (to Macedonius), all of which dwell on topics of relevance to an imperial administrator or indeed a local grandee involved in local public office, and two on aspects of household management (οἰκονομία), marriage and bringing up children—the latter to Sopater, who was in need of such advice, as the father of two sons. Thus are all three of the traditional subdivisions of the ethical branch of philosophy given at least some attention.

The subject of physics, or metaphysics, is dealt with, in fact, only incidentally to a topic that straddles the areas of ethics and physics, that

---

between the "civic" levels of virtue set out in the *Republic* as opposed to the "cathartic" or purificatory level mentioned in the *Phaedo*.

of fate, providence, and free will. This latter topic is dealt with most fully in the letter to Macedonius (*Letter* 8), but also, more briefly, in *Letter* 11, to Poemenius, and *Letter* 12, to Sopater. The metaphysical system revealed in the letter to Macedonius is fairly simple by Iamblichean standards but still involves a One, as supreme principle, generating a realm of primal Being (τὸ πρώτως ὄν), which is also that of Intellect and which constitutes the sum total of the multiplicity of Forms. This multiplicity is in turn referred back to "the principle of Multiplicity" (ἡ τῶν πολλῶν ἀρχή), which may be identified as the Indefinite Dyad. Below this in turn is a World Soul, and below that the realm of Nature, which may be taken as being that aspect of the World Soul that concerns itself with the generation and administration of the physical world. It is this latter level of being that we find to be the sphere of operations of Fate (εἱμαρμένη). It is defined at the end of fragment 1 of *Letter* 8 as "the one order [τάξις] that comprehends in itself all other orders."

What emerges from this is to all appearances a strictly determined world, on the Stoic model—as indeed one finds also in Plotinus (e.g., *Enn.* 3.2–3); but Iamblichus is also at pains to emphasize (in frg. 2) that the soul *in itself*, insofar as it emancipates itself from worldly influences and concerns, "contains within itself a free and independent life." In fragment 3 this concept is developed as follows:

> It is the life lived in accordance with intellect and that cleaves to the gods that we must train ourselves to live; for this is the only life that admits of the untrammeled authority of the soul, frees us from the bonds of necessity, and allows us to live a life no longer mortal, but one that is divine and filled by the will of the gods with divine benefits.

This is in fact more or less in accord with the doctrine of Plotinus, who also holds that what is for him the "higher" soul is free from the bonds of Fate, though it is really only free to assent to the order of the universe. For Iamblichus, Fate itself is dependent on Providence, which is the benign force guiding the higher, intelligible realm of reality. In fragment 4, their relationship is set out as follows:

> For indeed, to speak generally, the movements of destiny around the cosmos are assimilated to the immaterial and intellectual activities and circuits, and its order is assimilated to the good order of the intelligible and transcendent realm. And the secondary causes are dependent on the primary causes, and the multiplicity attendant upon generation on the undivided substance, and the whole sum of things subject to Fate is

thus connected to the dominance of Providence. In its very substance, then, Fate is enmeshed with Providence, and Fate exists by virtue of the existence of Providence, and it derives its existence from it and within its ambit."[10]

We find, then, in the *Letter to Macedonius* a fairly comprehensive picture of a simplified version of Neoplatonic metaphysics, suitable to a popular context, but yet not at odds with Iamblichus's deepest insights; this will be true of the doctrines set forth in the *Letters* as a whole. Iamblichus is not here, as we have said, concerned to lay out his full philosophical system but rather to bring the solace of philosophy to a range of educated laypeople and beyond them, no doubt, to a wider public, who were intended as the ultimate audience for these letters. We do not, of course, know precisely under what circumstances these letters were collected, but it is a fair inference that Iamblichus himself is envisaging such a fate for them, and to that extent they are intended to fulfill the role of an introduction to philosophy.[11]

5. Characteristics of Style and Vocabulary

Iamblichus's biographer Eunapius is on record as remarking that his subject, in respect of style, "did not sacrifice to the Graces" (*Vit. phil.* 458), and this evaluation would certainly seem to be borne out by a number of the verbatim fragments that still remain of his more technical treatises, as well as by the surviving *De mysteriis*, which, notwithstanding its great interest, is work of considerable turgidity. Even the prose style of the works making up the "Pythagorean Sequence," such as the *Pythagoric Life*,[12] leaves much to be desired. But this verdict does not seem to be so justified in respect of the *Letters*—as indeed befits their popular nature.

---

10. In *Letter 11*, to Poemenius, we actually find an assertion of the benign guidance of Fate by the gods, to an extent that seems to accord more with Christian theology than with Platonist philosophy.

11. The two testimonia provide evidence that, as one would have expected, the *Letters* were available in the sixth-century (and presumably also fifth-century) Academy as a collection. Such a volume may have been put together by Iamblichus himself in old age, but more probably by a pupil, such as Sopater or Eustathius, after his death.

12. John M. Dillon and Jackson Hershbell, eds., *Iamblichus: On the Pythagorean Way of Life* (SBLTT 29. Atlanta: Scholars Press, 1991).

Not that there are not occasional runs of parallel clauses or epithets such as are characteristic of his more technical treatises, but they are thankfully not a dominant feature.

On the other hand, we find a number of lively images and turns of phrase, together with some employment of literary and mythological allusions. The whole of the fragment *To Dexippus, On Dialectic* may serve as a good example of what Iamblichus is capable of in this regard:

> It was some god, in truth, who revealed dialectic and sent it down to men; as some say, Hermes, the god of rational discourse, who bears in his hands its symbol, of two snakes looking toward each other; but as the acknowledged masters of philosophy maintain, it is the eldest of the Muses, Calliope, who has provided the unshakeable and irrefutable firmness of reasoning, which shines forth "with honey-sweet modesty." And as the facts themselves demonstrate, the God in Delphi himself, in Heraclitus's words, "not speaking out, nor yet concealing, but signifying" his prophecies, rouses up those who hearken to his utterances to dialectical enquiry, on the basis of which they discerned ambiguity and homonymy, and the ferreting out of every double meaning kindled in them the light of knowledge. This indeed was something well discerned by Themistocles, who, in duly unraveling the riddle of the "wooden wall," indisputably established himself as the cause of salvation for the Greeks. And akin to these also are the feats of dialectic of the God in Branchidae, revealing clearly the procedure of induction, when he says, "No swift-flying arrow, nor lyre, nor ship, nor anything else would ever attain a useful end without use based on knowledge."

We find here the use of both mythological and literary allusions to reinforce his claim for the fundamental importance of dialectic. In the *Letter to Arete* also we find some fine turns of phrase and mythological and literary allusions: an allegorization of Bellerophon's slaying of the Chimaera, and Perseus's of the Gorgon, as well as a quotation from the Cynic Crates that may in fact be a line of iambic verse. The *Letter to Sopater on Bringing Up Children* makes much use, not unreasonably, of references to Plato's *Laws* and engages in some lively writing as well.

It cannot be denied, however, that there are also many passages in these letters that give some credence to Eunapius's evaluation quoted above. Iamblichus is prone to long runs of parallel phrases or clauses, in his efforts to define some concept or other, that make one long for a full stop. One example will suffice, from the *Letter to Sopater on Fate*:

> The essence of Fate subsists entirely within the ambit of Nature, by which latter I mean the immanent causal principle of the cosmos, and that which immanently comprises the totality of causes of the realm of generation, such as the higher essences and orders comprehend within themselves in a transcendent mode. That life, therefore, which relates to body and the rational principle which is concerned with generation, the forms-in-matter and Matter itself, and the creation that is put together out of these elements, and that motion which produces change in all of these, and that Nature which administers in an orderly way all things that come into being, and the beginnings and ends and creations of Nature, and the combinations of these with each other and their progressions from beginning to end—all these go to make up the essence of Fate.

There is little that is graceful in this, certainly, but Sopater was a serious philosopher, and doubtless he could take it. At all events, Iamblichus is shown to be capable of fine writing when he puts his mind to it—as indeed befits the author of a treatise Περὶ κρίσεως ἀρίστου λόγου, "On Judging the Best Type of Speech."[13]

6. A Note on the Text

The basis for our text as we present it here is the 1958 reprint of Kurt Wachsmuth and Otto Hense's edition of the *Anthology* of John of Stobi.[14] The same is true for the apparatus, with the only exception that we left out those notes that were of minor importance to the meaning of the text. Given the fact that the fragments of Iamblichus's letters are handed down to us solely through John of Stobi's work, and since it was not our aim to edit his anthology, we think that our approach is justifiable. The following list of abbreviations for the manuscript tradition of John of Stobi's work is compiled on the basis of that of Wachsmuth and Hense.

---

13. Attested by Syrianus, *In Hermogenem* 1; Hugo Rabe, ed., *Syriani in Hermogenem commentaria* [2 vols. in 1; BT; Leipzig: Teubner, 1892–93], 1:9,11). In the context, we may presume that this was a treatise on rhetoric rather than anything philosophical.

14. On the manuscript tradition of John of Stobi, see now Federica Ciccolella, "Stobaios, Ioannes," in *Geschichte der antiken Texte: Autoren- und Werklexikon* (ed. Manfred Landfester; Der Neue Pauly Supplemente 2; Stuttgart: Metzler, 2007), 563–65.

A	codex Parisinus prior "Florilegii," cod. Graec. 1984, fourteenth century
B	codex Parisinus alter "Florilegii," cod. Graec. 1985, sixteenth century
Br	codex Bruxellensis, n. 11360, fourteenth/fifteenth century
F	codex Farnesis, III D 15, fourteenth century
L	codex Laurentianus sacri profani florilegii, Florentinus plutei VIII n. 22, fourteenth century
M	codex Mendozae Escurialensis LXXXX (Σ II 14), eleventh/twelfth century
M^d	codicis Escurialensis collatio Dindorfiana
P	codex Parisinus "Eclogarum" n. 2129, fifteenth century
S	codex Vindobonensis cod. philos. et philol. Gr. LXVII, eleventh century
Tr.	editio Trincavelliana Florilegii ex codice Marciano (class. IV cod. XXIX, fifteenth/sixteenth century) expressa, Venice 1535 (or 1536),[15] editio princeps

Our apparatus also comprises the names of philologists who made conjectures on John of Stobi's text. Some of them apparently were communicated to Wachsmuth and Hense rather informally. Therefore, we left Wachsmuth and Hense's remarks unchanged. We added just a few conjectures.

---

15. On the problem regarding the date of this edition, see Beate Czapla, "Der Kuß des geflügelten Eros: Die Darstellungen des Liebesgottes in Moschos I und Bion Aposp. XIII Gow als hellenistische Kontrafakturen des γλυκύπικρον ἀμάχανον ὄρπετον," in *Beyond the Canon* (ed. Annette Harder, Remco F. Regtuit, and Gerry C. Wakker; Hellenistica Groningana 11; Leuven: Peeters, 2006), 61–82, here 79 n. 64.

Text and Translation

Letter 1
Πρὸς Ἀγρίππαν περὶ ἀρχῆς

Fragment 1
Stobaeus, *Anth.* 4.5.76
4:223,7–12 Hense

Ἐπίφθονος εἶναι δοκεῖ τοῖς πολλοῖς ἡ ὑπεροχὴ τῆς ἀρχῆς, καὶ τὸ ὑπέρογκον μισητὸν αὐτοῖς καθίσταται· ἀλλ' ὅταν χρηστότητι καὶ φιλανθρωπίᾳ κραθῇ τὸ σεμνὸν καὶ αὐστηρὸν τῆς ἐπικρατείας, ἐμμελὲς καὶ πρᾶον καὶ προσηνὲς καὶ εὐπρόσιτον καθίσταται. καὶ τοῦτο μάλιστα τὸ εἶδος
5 ἡγεμονίας φιλεῖται ὑπὸ τῶν ἀρχομένων.

1 ἀρετῆς S

Fragment 2
Stobaeus, *Anth.* 4.5.77
4:223,14–224,7 Hense

Λέγεται μὲν εἶναι πάντων βασιλεὺς ὁ νόμος· ὁ δὲ αὐτὸς δοκεῖ καὶ προστάττειν τἀγαθὰ καὶ τἀναντία ἀπαγορεύειν. τί δὴ οὖν οἰόμεθα τὴν παρισουμένην πρὸς αὐτὸν εὐνομίαν οἵῳ δὴ κάλλει τινὶ προέχειν μεγέθει τε ἡλίκῳ [δικαιοσύνῃ] ὑπερβάλλειν πάντα πράγματα; ὅσα γὰρ δήπου καὶ οἷα
5 γένη καὶ εἴδη τῶν ἀρετῶν ἐστι, κατὰ τοσαῦτα καὶ τοιαῦτα διήκει κάλλη τὰ τῶν νόμων ἐπιτάγματα, καὶ δὴ καθ' ὅλας τὰς διοικήσεις τῶν πόλεων καὶ τοὺς ὅλους τῶν ἀνθρώπων βίους διατείνει τὸ ἀπ' αὐτῶν ὄφελος. ἔστι μὲν οὖν κοινὸν ἀγαθὸν ὁ νόμος, καὶ ἄνευ τούτου οὐδὲν ἄν ποτε γένοιτο τῶν ἀγαθῶν· δεῖ γε μὴν τὸν προϊστάμενον τῶν νόμων ἄρχοντα εἰλικρινῶς
10 ἀποκεκαθαρμένον εἶναι πρὸς αὐτὴν τὴν ἄκραν τῶν νόμων ὀρθότητα, καὶ μήτε παραγωγαῖς ἢ φενακισμοῖς ἐξαπατᾶσθαι δι' ἄγνοιαν, μήτε βιαζομένοις τισὶ συγχωρεῖν, μήτε ἀδίκῳ προφάσει μηδεμίᾳ δελεάζεσθαι. τὸν γὰρ σωτῆρα καὶ φύλακα τῶν νόμων ἀδιάφθορον εἶναι δεῖ εἰς δύναμιν ἀνθρωπίνην.

4 δικαιοσύνῃ eiciendum esse vidit Bake ad Cic. de legg. I 6,18

Letter 1

To Agrippa, On Ruling

Fragment 1
The absolute superiority associated with rule appears offensive to the multitude, and the pomp and circumstance of it is hateful to them; but when the solemnity and austerity of rule is blended with nobility of character and sympathy for one's fellow human beings, then it makes itself felt as harmonious and mild and pleasant and approachable; and it is this type of leadership that is most of all loved by the ruled.

Fragment 2
Law is said to be the "king of all." This it is that is held to prescribe good actions and forbid their opposites. Well then, with what beauty in our view does a lawfulness that is coordinated with this exceed, and with what sort of greatness does it overmatch, all other things? For surely, in respect of however many and whatever kinds of types and classes of moral excellence there are, so many and various are the beauties that the prescriptions of the laws extend to, and their benefit permeates all the administrations of cities and all the lives of individuals. So law is a good for all in common, and without it none of the other goods could come about. Consequently, the ruler who is placed in responsibility for the laws must have a completely pure insight into the absolute correctness of the laws and should neither be led astray, through ignorance, by deceptions or frauds, nor should he yield to any show of force, nor be deceived by any unjust excuse. For the preserver and guardian of the laws should be as immune from corruption as is humanly possible.

Letter 2
Πρὸς Ἀνατόλιον περὶ δικαιοσύνης

Fragment 1
Stobaeus, *Anth.* 3.9.35
3:358,5–8 Hense

Ἐπ' αὐτὸ δὴ τὸ τῶν ὅλων ἀρετῶν τέλος καὶ τὴν συναγωγὴν αὐτῶν συμπασῶν, ἐν ᾗ δὴ πᾶσαι ἔνεισι συλλήβδην κατὰ τὸν παλαιὸν λόγον, γένοιτο ἄν τις εἰς τὴν δικαιοσύνην ἀγόμενος.

2 ἔνεισι S A Br, ἔν εἰσι M^d

Fragment 2
Stobaeus, *Anth.* 3.9.36
3:358,10–17 Hense

Ἐν δὲ τῷ ἀνθρωπίνῳ βίῳ διανομὴ τῶν κατ' ἀξίαν ἔργων τε καὶ τιμῶν καὶ τῶν ἄλλων τῶν ἐπιβαλλόντων ἑκάστοις ὑφίστησι τὴν εἰς τὸν ἀνθρώπινον βίον τείνουσαν δικαιοσύνην. ἔργα τοίνυν τῇ δικαιοσύνῃ τὰ πρόσφορα καὶ ἐπιτηδεύματα εἴη ἄν, ὅσα κοινωνικὰ καὶ ἥμερα τυγχάνει καὶ εὐσύμβολα καὶ
5 εὐσυνάλλακτα καὶ ὠφέλιμα, τῶν βλαβερῶν κωλυτικὰ διαπράξεων, τῶν δ' ἐναντίων τὴν ὅλην κατάστασιν εὐτρεπῆ παρασκευάζοντα.

4 τυγχάνει S M^d, τυγχάνοι A ‖ 6 εὐτρεπῆ M^d: εὐπρεπῆ S A

Letter 2
To Anatolius, On Justice

Fragment 1
It is to the very culmination of all the virtues and the summation of all of them, in which, indeed, as the ancient account tells us, they are all present together, that one would come by being led to justice.

Fragment 2
In the life of human beings, it is the apportionment of befitting actions and honors, and all the other things that relate to the individual, that constitutes that justice which pertains to human life. The activities and practices proper to justice would then be such as tend to community feeling and mildness, to the observance of contracts and agreements, and to the common advantage, being restrictive of harmful activities, while bringing about a favorable climate for the comprehensive establishment of activities of the opposite sort.

Letter 3
Πρὸς Ἀρετὴν περὶ σωφροσύνης

Fragment 1
Stobaeus, *Anth.* 3.5.9
3:257,13–258,4 Hense

Τὰ αὐτὰ δὴ οὖν καὶ περὶ πασῶν τῶν δυνάμεων τῆς ψυχῆς ἀποφαίνομαι, τὴν συμμετρίαν αὐτῶν πρὸς ἀλλήλας καὶ εὐταξίαν θυμοῦ τε καὶ ἐπιθυμίας καὶ λόγου κατὰ τὴν προσήκουσαν ἑκάστῳ τάξιν εὐκοσμίαν· καὶ τούτων ἡ τοῦ ἄρχειν τε καὶ ἄρχεσθαι ἐν δέοντι γιγνομένη διανομὴ σωφροσύνη ἂν εἴη
5 πολυειδής.

3 ἑκάστῳ M^d A Tr.: ἑκάστου L

Fragment 2
Stobaeus, *Anth.* 3.5.45
3:270,12–16 Hense

Πᾶσα μὲν γὰρ ἀρετὴ τὸ θνητοειδὲς μὲν ἀτιμάζει, τὸ δὲ ἀθάνατον ἀσπάζεται· πολὺ δὲ διαφερόντως ἡ σωφροσύνη ταύτην ἔχει τὴν σπουδήν, ἅτε δὴ τὰς προσηλούσας τῷ σώματι τὴν ψυχὴν ἡδονὰς ἀτιμάζουσα, καὶ ἐν ἁγνοῖς βάθροις βεβῶσα, ὥς φησι Πλάτων.

2 πολὺ (sic ut coniecerat Gesn.² p. 68 mrg) L A Br: πολλὴ M, inde vulg.

Fragment 3
Stobaeus, *Anth.* 3.5.46
3:270,18–271,6 Hense

Πῶς γὰρ ἡ σωφροσύνη τελέους ἡμᾶς οὐ ποιεῖ, τὸ ἀτελὲς καὶ ἐμπαθὲς ὅλον ἀφ' ἡμῶν ἐξορίζουσα; γνοίης δ' ἂν ὡς τοῦτο οὕτως ἔχει, τὸν Βελλεροφόντην ἐννοήσας, ὃς μετὰ τῆς κοσμιότητος συναγωνιζόμενος τὴν Χίμαιραν καὶ τὸ θηριῶδες καὶ ἄγριον καὶ ἀνήμερον φῦλον πᾶν ἀνεῖλεν. ὅλως γὰρ ἡ τῶν παθῶν

Letter 3
To Arete, On Self-Control

Fragment 1
I would make the same statement also about all the powers of the soul, that orderliness consists in the symmetry of these with each other, and the correct arrangement of the spirited element and the libido and the reason, in accordance with the ranking proper to each; and it is the bringing about of a suitable apportionment among these of ruling and being ruled that might be termed the multiform virtue of self-control.

Fragment 2
For every virtue holds in contempt the mortal element and embraces the immortal, but in a very special way self-control has this aim, inasmuch as it despises the pleasures that "nail" us "to the body" (*Phd.* 83D) and "stands upon holy foundations," as Plato says (*Phdr.* 254B)

Fragment 3
For how would self-control not render us perfect, seeing as it eliminates from our make-up all that is imperfect and subject to passion? You might recognize that this is so if you call to mind Bellerophon, who, with good order as his ally, destroyed the Chimaera and the whole tribe of the beastly and savage and ungentle. For in general the immoderate

5 ἄμετρος ἐπικράτεια οὐδὲ ἀνθρώπους ἐφίησιν εἶναι τοὺς ἀνθρώπους, πρὸς δὲ τὴν ἀλόγιστον αὐτοὺς ἕλκει καὶ θηριώδη καὶ ἄτακτον.

1 ἀτελὲς M^d A: εὐτελὲς L ‖ **3** συναγωνιζόμενος Meineke: συναγωνιζομένης ms. ‖ **5** ἀφίησιν L M^d A: corr. Meineke

Fragment 4
Stobaeus, *Anth*. 3.5.47
3:271,8–15 Hense

Ἡ δὲ μέτροις ὡρισμένοις κατέχουσα τὰς ἡδονὰς εὐταξία σῴζει μὲν οἴκους σῴζει δὲ πόλεις κατὰ τὴν Κράτητος γνώμην· ἔτι δὲ πλησιάζει πως ἤδη πρὸς τὸ τῶν θεῶν εἶδος. τοιγὰρ οὖν Περσεὺς ἐπ' αὐτὸ τὸ ἀκρότατον ἐλαύνων τῆς σωφροσύνης [ἀγαθὸν] ἡγουμένης τῆς Ἀθηνᾶς ἀπέκοψε τὴν Γοργόνα, τὴν εἰς
5 τὴν ὕλην οἶμαι καθέλκουσαν καὶ ἀπολιθοῦσαν τοὺς ἀνθρώπους ἀνοήτῳ τῶν παθημάτων πλησμονῇ.

4 ἀγαθὸν secludi vult Meineke

Fragment 5
Stobaeus, *Anth*. 3.5.48
3:271,17–21 Hense

Ὅτι τοίνυν κρηπὶς τῆς ἀρετῆς, ὡς ἔλεγε Σωκράτης, ἡ ἐγκράτειά ἐστι τῆς γλυκυθυμίας· κόσμος δὲ τῶν ἀγαθῶν πάντων ἡ σωφροσύνη θεωρεῖται, ὥσπερ δὴ ἀπεφήνατο Πλάτων. ἀσφάλεια δὲ τῶν καλλίστων ἕξεων ἡ αὐτή ἐστιν ἀρετή, ὥσπερ ἐγὼ λέγω.

3 ἕξεων L, ἕξεων M^d, ἐξ ὧν A

Fragment 6
Stobaeus, *Anth*. 3.5.49
3:271,23–272,3 Hense

Ὃ δ' ἐστὶν ὄντως ὁμολογούμενον θαρρῶν διισχυρίζομαι, ὅτι δὴ δι' ὅλων τῶν ἀρετῶν τὸ κάλλος διατείνει τῆς σωφροσύνης καὶ συναρμόζει τὰς πάσας ἀρετὰς κατὰ μίαν ἁρμονίαν συμμετρίαν τε αὐταῖς καὶ κρᾶσιν πρὸς

domination of the passions does not permit men to be men but drags them toward the nature that is irrational and bestial and disordered.

Fragment 4

The good order that contains the pleasures within measured bounds "saves households and save cities," according to the dictum of Crates; and further, it somehow brings us near to the form of the gods. Even so, then, did Perseus, ascending to the highest pinnacle of excellence in moderation, under the guidance of Athene, cut off the head of the Gorgon, which I take to be the power that drags men down into matter and petrifies them through mindless indulgence in the passions.

Fragment 5

The foundation of virtue, then, as Socrates used to say, is the control of self-indulgence; and self-control is viewed as the adornment of all goods, as Plato maintained. And this virtue is the surest guarantee of the finest habits of mind, as I would say myself.

Fragment 6

I have no hesitation in asserting what is truly a matter of general agreement, that the beauty of self-control extends throughout all the virtues, and harmonizes all the virtues into one accord, and instills into them symmetry and blending with one another. This being its nature,

ἀλλήλας ἐντίθησι. τοιαύτη δὴ οὖν οὖσα καὶ ἀφορμὴν παρέχει ταῖς ὅλαις
5 ὥστε ἐγγενέσθαι, καὶ ἐγγενομέναις αὐταῖς ἀσφαλῆ παρέχει σωτηρίαν.

Fragment 7
Stobaeus, *Anth.* 3.5.50
3:272,5-9 Hense

Καὶ ἡ τῶν ὡρῶν τοῦ ἐνιαυτοῦ σύστασις καὶ ἡ τῶν στοιχείων πρὸς ἄλληλα σύγκρασις συμφωνίαν ἀποσῴζει καλλίστην καὶ σώφρονα. καὶ τό γε πᾶν τοῦτο διὰ τὴν κοσμιότητα τῶν καλλίστων μέτρων κόσμος ἐπικαλεῖται.

---

2 σύγκρασις L M^d Br: ἔγκρασις A | τὸ γε L A: τότε (vel τό τε) M^d Br ‖ **3** μέτρων M^d A Br: ὡρῶν teste Gaisfordo; μερῶν Cobet mnemos. IX p. 110.

it both provides a stimulus to all of them to come into being and, when they are established, assures their firm preservation.

Fragment 7

Both the arrangement of the seasons of the year and the blending of the elements with one another preserve a most fair and self-controlled harmony. And so this universe is called a cosmos (i.e., an ordered whole) by reason of the good order of its fairest measures.

Letter 4
Πρὸς Ἀσφάλιον περὶ φρονήσεως

Stobaeus, *Anth.* 3.3.26,
3:201,17–202,17 Hense

Τὴν ἡγεμόν' οὖσαν τῶν ἀρετῶν φρόνησιν καὶ χρωμένην αὐταῖς ὅλαις, καθάπερ ὄμμα νοερόν, τάξεις τε καὶ μέτρα αὐτῶν κατὰ τὴν ἐγκαιροτάτην διάθεσιν εὖ διακοσμοῦσαν ἐπιδείκνυσιν ὁ λόγος ὑπ' αὐγὰς ἐν τῷ παρόντι. αὕτη τοίνυν προηγουμένην μὲν παραδέχεται τὴν ἀπογέννησιν ἀπὸ τοῦ
5 καθαροῦ καὶ τελείου νοῦ· γενομένη δ' οὕτως εἰς αὐτὸν τὸν νοῦν ἀποβλέπει καὶ τελειοῦται ἀπ' αὐτοῦ μέτρον τε καὶ παράδειγμα αὐτὸν ἔχων κάλλιστον τῶν ἐν αὐτῇ πασῶν ἐνεργειῶν. εἰ δέ τίς ἐστι καὶ πρὸς θεοὺς ἡμῖν κοινωνία, διὰ ταύτης μάλιστα τῆς ἀρετῆς αὕτη συνίσταται, καὶ κατὰ ταύτην διαφερόντως πρὸς αὐτοὺς ἀφομοιούμεθα· ἀγαθῶν τε καὶ συμφερόντων καὶ καλῶν καὶ τῶν
10 ἐναντίων διάγνωσις ἀπὸ ταύτης ἡμῖν πάρεστιν, ἔργων τε προσηκόντων κρίσις καὶ κατόρθωσις δι' αὐτῆς κατευθύνεται. καὶ συλλήβδην φάναι, κυβερνητική τίς ἐστι τῶν ἀνθρώπων καὶ τῆς ὅλης ἐν αὐτοῖς διατάξεως ἀρχηγός, πόλεις τε καὶ οἴκους καὶ τὸν ἴδιον ἑκάστου βίον εἰς παράδειγμα τὸ θεῖον ἀναφέρουσα διαζωγραφεῖ κατὰ τὴν ἀρίστην ὁμοιότητα, τὸ μὲν ἐξαλείφουσα, τὸ δὲ
15 ἐναπομοργνυμένη, τὰ δὲ ἀμφότερα συμμέτρως ἀπεικάζουσα. εἰκότως ἄρα καὶ θεοειδεῖς ἀπεργάζεται τοὺς ἔχοντας αὐτὴν ἡ φρόνησις.

---

1 ὅλαις] ὕλαις A || 2 κατὰ τὴν Dillon, καὶ τὴν mss. | ἐγκαιροτάτην M^d A Br εὐκαιροτάτην Tr. || 3 ὁ λ.] ὅλον Tr. | ὑπ' αὐγὰς A (?): ὑπαυγὲς M^d Tr. Br id est ὑπ' αὐγαῖς || 4 προηγουμένην Dillon, προηγουμένη mss. || 6 τελειοῦται Br: τελεοῦται M^d A Tr. | ἔχων Dillon, ἔχει mss.

Letter 4
To Asphalius, On Wisdom

It is wisdom, which dominates all the other virtues and makes use of all of them, like an eye of the intellect ordering well their ranks and proportions according to the most apt arrangement, that discourse displays before our gaze at the present. This, then, receives its existence principally from the pure and perfect intellect. Once generated, however, it contemplates the intellect itself and derives its perfection from it, possessing it as a most noble measure and model for all the activities that take place within it. And if there is any community between us and the gods, it is constituted most of all through this virtue, and it is in accordance with it that we are particularly assimilated to them. It is from this that we acquire discernment of what is good and advantageous and noble and their opposites, and through this that judgment concerning, and accomplishment of, appropriate acts is achieved. And in sum, it has the characteristic of directing men and administering the whole structure of their relations with one another, and, in referring cities and households and the private life of each individual to a divine model, it portrays them in likeness to what is best, rubbing out something here, painting in something there, and in both cases bringing everything to a harmonious likeness. It is quite reasonable, therefore, to assert that wisdom renders those who possess it like unto god.

Letter 5
Πρὸς Δέξιππον περὶ διαλεκτικῆς

Stobaeus, *Anth.* 2.2.5
2:18,13–19,11 Wachsmuth

Θεὸς ἦν τις ὡς ἀληθῶς ὁ καταδείξας τὴν διαλεκτικὴν καὶ καταπέμψας τοῖς ἀνθρώποις· ὡς μὲν λέγουσί τινες, ὁ λόγιος Ἑρμῆς, ὁ φέρων ἐν ταῖν χεροῖν τὸ σύνθημα αὐτῆς ⟨τὸ⟩ τῶν εἰς ἀλλήλους ἀποβλεπόντων δρακόντων· ὡς δ' οἱ δεδοκιμασμένοι καὶ πρόκριτοι τῶν ἐν φιλοσοφίᾳ διατείνονται, ἡ τῶν Μουσῶν
5 πρεσβυτάτη Καλλιόπη τὴν ἄπταιστον ἀσφάλειαν τοῦ λόγου καὶ ἀνελέγκτον "αἰδοῖ μειλιχίῃ" διαπρέπουσαν παρέσχηκεν. ὡς δὲ τὰ ἔργα αὐτὰ δείκνυσιν, αὐτὸς ὁ ἐν Δελφοῖς θεὸς οὔτε λέγων καθ' Ἡράκλειτον, οὔτε κρύπτων ἀλλὰ σημαίνων τὰς μαντείας, ἐγείρει πρὸς διαλεκτικὴν διερεύνησιν τοὺς ἐπηκόους τῶν χρησμῶν, ἀφ' ἧς ἀμφιβολία τε καὶ ὁμωνυμία ἐκρίθησαν καὶ διττὸν πᾶν
10 ἀνερευνηθὲν φῶς ἐπιστήμης ἀνῆψεν· ὃ κατιδὼν καὶ Θεμιστοκλῆς καλῶς καὶ διερευνήσας δεόντως τὸ ξύλινον τεῖχος, αἴτιος ἀναμφισβητήτως κατέστη τῆς σωτηρίας τοῖς Ἕλλησιν. ἀδελφὰ δὲ τούτων καὶ ὁ ἐν Βραγχίδαις θεὸς ἐκφαίνει τῆς διαλεκτικῆς ἔργα, περιφανῆ τὴν ἐπαγωγὴν παραδηλῶν, ὅταν λέγῃ· "οὔτ' ἂν ὠκυπέτης ἰὸς οὔτε λύρη οὔτε νηῦς οὔτε ἄλλο οὐδὲν ἄνευ
15 ἐπιστημονικῆς χρήσιος γένοιτ' ἄν κοτε ὠφέλιμον."

---

3 τό add. Jacobs lect. Stob. p. 123 | ὡς ἀεὶ libri: ὡς δ' οἱ Jacobs l. s. (ὡς δὲ οἱ ἀεὶ Gesner) || 14–15 ναῦς et χρήσεως et ποτε libri: corr. Meineke

Letter 5
To Dexippus, On Dialectic

It was some god, in truth, who revealed dialectic and sent it down to men; as some say, Hermes, the god of rational discourse, who bears in his hands its symbol, of two snakes looking toward each other; but as the acknowledged masters of philosophy maintain, it is the eldest of the Muses, Calliope, who has provided the unshakeable and irrefutable firmness of reasoning, which shines forth "with honey-sweet modesty." And as the facts themselves demonstrate, the God in Delphi himself, in Heraclitus's words, "not speaking out, nor yet concealing, but signifying" his prophecies, rouses up those who hearken to his utterances to dialectical enquiry, on the basis of which they discerned ambiguity and homonymy, and the ferreting out of every double meaning kindled in them the light of knowledge. This indeed was something well discerned by Themistocles, who, in duly unraveling the riddle of the "wooden wall," indisputably established himself as the cause of salvation for the Greeks. And akin to these also are the feats of dialectic of the God in Branchidae, revealing clearly the procedure of induction, when he says, "No swift-flying arrow, nor lyre, nor ship, nor anything else would ever attain a useful end without use based on knowledge."

Letter 6
Πρὸς Δυσκόλιον περὶ ἀρχῆς (?)

Fragment 1
Stobaeus, *Anth.* 4.5.74
4:222,7-18 Hense

Προηγεῖται δ' ὡς ἀληθῶς ἄρχων μειζόνως αὐτῶν καὶ ἔτι βελτιόνως, ⟨ὃς⟩ τὴν μεγαλοπρεπῆ δόσιν τῶν ἀγαθῶν παρέχει χορηγίαν τε ἄπλετον τοῦ βίου καὶ σωτηρίαν πλείστην καὶ ζωῆς ῥᾳστώνην ἐντίθησιν. καὶ γὰρ δὴ καὶ τοῦτό ἐστι τέλος ἄρχοντος σπουδαίου τοὺς ἀρχομένους ποιεῖν εὐδαίμονας· καὶ τότε
5 δὴ διαφερόντως εὐσθενεῖ ὁ προεστηκὼς τῶν ὑφ' ἑαυτοῦ διοικουμένων, ὅταν οἱ ἐπιτρέψαντες αὐτῷ ἑαυτοὺς μακαρίως διάγωσιν. οὐ γὰρ δὴ κεχώρισται τὸ κοινὸν συμφέρον τοῦ ἰδίου· πολὺ δὲ μᾶλλον ἐν τῷ ὅλῳ καὶ τὸ καθ' ἕκαστα λυσιτελοῦν περιέχεται καὶ σῴζεται ἐν τῷ παντὶ τὸ κατὰ μέρος ἐπί τε τῶν ζῴων καὶ τῶν πόλεων καὶ τῶν ἄλλων φύσεων.

1 βέλτιον ὡς (ὥστε A) libri: corr. et suppl. Thomas Herm. XIV | ὅστις Hirschig

Fragment 2
Stobaeus, *Anth.* 4.5.75
4:222,20-223,5 Hense

Ἄγαμαι δ' ἔγωγε καὶ τὴν μεγαλοφροσύνην καὶ τὴν μεγαλοπρέπειαν ἐν ἅπασι τοῖς τῆς ἀρχῆς ἔργοις, καὶ διαφερόντως ἐν ταῖς τῶν ἀνθρώπων εὐεργεσίαις, ὅταν μήτε ἀκριβολογῶνται μήτε φείδωνταί τινος ἐν ταῖς δόσεσι μήτε ὥσπερ ἐν πλάστιγγι ζυγοῦ ἴσα ἀντὶ ἴσων ἀντικαταλλάττωνται,
5 εὐγενῶς δὲ τὰς χάριτας ὀρέγωσι, μὴ μόνον ἐκ πίθου αὐτὰς προχέοντες, ὡς οἱ ποιηταὶ λέγουσιν, μηδ' ἄλλοις τισὶν ὀργάνοις τοιούτοις εἴσω κατεχομένας, γυμνὰς δὲ καὶ ἀπαρακαλύπτους καὶ χωρὶς τῶν ἔξωθεν παραπετασμάτων συνεχεῖς ἐχομένας ἀλλήλων προτείνωσι χρηστῶς καὶ εὐμενῶς, οἷα δὴ καὶ χαρίεντα. τῶν χαρίτων γὰρ δὴ τοιοῦτον κόσμον στέφανον ἂν εἰκότως εἴποιμι
10 τῆς ἀρχῆς.

5 δὲ Meineke: τε libri

Letter 6
To Dyscolius, On Ruling (?)

Fragment 1
He guides people more effectively, and even better than that, as a true leader, who provides a generous donation of good things and an unstinting supply of the means of life and establishes a maximum degree of safety and leisure in living. For this, after all, is the aim of a good ruler, to cause his subjects to flourish; and it is precisely then that a leader is distinguished in power above those that he administers, when those who have entrusted themselves to him enjoy a blessed existence. For the common good is not to be separated from the individual good; on the contrary, the individual advantage is subsumed within that of the whole, and the particular is preserved in the universal, in the case of both living things and states and all other natural entities.

Fragment 2
For my part, I respect high-mindedness and generosity in all the activities of government, and especially in the area of benefactions, when rulers are not exact nor sparing in their donations to someone, nor reckon up as in a scale equal for equal in their exchanges, but rather put forth their acts of generosity with nobility, not just "pouring them out from a jar," as the poets say, nor having them confined within any other such receptacles, but rather extending them naked and uncovered and free of any external covering conditions, following continually one upon another, honestly and with goodwill, in a way that is indeed gratifying. Such a program of benefactions I would certainly term, and reasonably so, the "crown" of an administration.

Letter 7
Πρὸς Εὐστάθιον περὶ μουσικῆς

Stobaeus, *Anth.* 2.31.117
2:229,6-8 Wachsmuth

... <ἔ>ν ἐκεῖνο εἰδότας, ὡς αἵ τε μεγάλαι φύσεις τὰ μεγάλα κακὰ γεννῶσι διαφθαρεῖσαι καὶ τὰ κράτιστα ἐπιτηδεύματα πάντως ἐστὶ βλαβερώτατα ἐπὶ τὸ κακὸν ῥέψαντα.

---

1 ν L

Letter 7
To Eustathius, On Music

... knowing this <one> thing, that great natures produce great evils when corrupted, and the greatest enterprises are in all cases the most harmful when they go to the bad.

Letter 8
Πρὸς Μακεδόνιον περὶ εἱμαρμένης

Fragment 1
Stobaeus, *Anth.* 1.5.17
1:80,11–81,6 Wachsmuth

Πάντα μὲν τὰ ὄντα τῷ ἑνί ἐστιν ὄντα· καὶ γὰρ αὐτὸ τὸ πρώτως ὂν ἀπὸ τοῦ ἑνὸς ἐξ ἀρχῆς παράγεται, πολὺ δὲ διαφερόντως τὰ ὅλα αἴτια τῷ ἑνὶ τὸ δύνασθαι ποιεῖν παραδέχεται καὶ κατὰ μίαν συμπλοκὴν συνέχεται καὶ συναναφέρεται τῇ τῶν πολλῶν ἀρχῇ προϋπάρχοντα. κατὰ δὴ τοῦτον τὸν
5 λόγον καὶ τῶν περὶ τὴν φύσιν αἰτίων, πολυειδῶν ὄντων καὶ πολυμερίστων, ἠρτημένων τε ἀπὸ πλειόνων ἀρχῶν, ἀπὸ μιᾶς ὅλης αἰτίας τὸ πλῆθος ἐκκρέμαται, κατὰ μίαν δὲ σύνδεσιν πάντα πρὸς ἄλληλα συμπλέκεται καὶ εἰς ἓν ἀνήκει τὸ περιεκτικώτατον τῆς αἰτίας κράτος ὁ σύνδεσμος τῶν πλειόνων αἰτίων. οὗτος τοίνυν εἷς εἱρμὸς ⟨οὐ⟩ συμπεφορημένος ἐστὶν ἀπὸ
10 τοῦ πλήθους, οὐδ' ἐπισυνισταμένην ἀπὸ τῆς συμπλοκῆς ποιεῖται τὴν ἕνωσιν, οὐδὲ διαπεφόρηται ἐν τοῖς καθ' ἕκαστα· κατὰ δὲ τὴν προηγουμένην καὶ προτεταγμένην αὐτῶν τῶν αἰτίων μίαν συμπλοκὴν ἐπιτελεῖ πάντα καὶ συνδεῖ ἐν ἑαυτῷ καὶ πρὸς αὐτὸν μονοειδῶς ἀνάγει. μίαν οὖν τάξιν, πάσας τάξεις ὁμοῦ περιλαβοῦσαν ἐν αὐτῇ, τὴν εἱμαρμένην ἀφοριστέον.

1 πρώτως F P², πρῶτος P¹, πρῶτον Canter, Wachsmuth ‖ 2 ὅλα P, ὄντα F ‖ 4 προϋπάρχοντι F P: corr. Usener ‖ 5 αἰτίων pro αἰτιῶν corr. Meineke ‖ 8 αἰτίας P, σοφίας F ‖ 9 αἰτίων pro αἰτιῶν corr. Meineke | εἱρμός corr. Meineke pro εἰργμός | οὐ add. Usener ‖ 12 τῆς αἰτίας F P: τῶν αἰτίων Wachsmuth, τῶν αἰτιῶν Heeren ‖ 13 συνδεῖν F P: corr. Canter | αὐτόν F P: corr. Heeren ‖ 14 αὐτῇ F P: corr. Heeren

Fragment 2
Stobaeus, *Anth.* 2.8.43
2:173,5–17 Wachsmuth

Οὐσία ἐστὶν ἄϋλος ἡ τῆς ψυχῆς καθ' ἑαυτήν, ἀσώματος, ἀγέννητος πάντη καὶ ἀνώλεθρος, παρ' ἑαυτῆς ἔχουσα τὸ εἶναι καὶ τὸ ζῆν, αὐτοκίνητος παντελῶς καὶ ἀρχὴ τῆς φύσεως καὶ τῶν ὅλων κινήσεων. αὕτη δὴ οὖν καθ'

Letter 8
To Macedonius, On Fate

Fragment 1

All things that exist, exist by virtue of the One, and indeed the primal level of Being itself is produced in the beginning from the One, and in a very special way the general causal principles receive their power of action from the One, and are held together by it in a single embrace, and are borne back together to the first principle of multiplicity, as pre-existing in it. And in accordance with this, the multitude also of causal principles in nature, which are multiform and fragmented, and dependent on a number of (immediate) sources, yet derive from one general causal principle, and all are interwoven with each other according to a single principle of combination, and this combination of many causal principles relate back to one source, the most comprehensive controlling principle of causality. This single chain is not a mere jumble put together from Multiplicity, nor does it constitute a unity formed simply as a result of such combination, nor is it dissipated into individual entities; but rather in accordance with the guiding and prearranged single combination of the causal principles themselves, it brings all things to completion and binds them within itself, and leads them upwards unitarily to itself. Thus Fate is to be defined as the one order that comprehends in itself all other orders.

Fragment 2

The essence of the soul in itself is immaterial, incorporeal, completely exempt from generation and destruction, possessing of itself existence and life, entirely self-moved and first principle of nature and of motions in general. This entity, in virtue of being such as it is, also con-

ὅσον ἐστὶ τοιαύτη, καὶ τὴν αὐτεξούσιον καὶ τὴν ἀπόλυτον περιείληφεν ἐν
ἑαυτῇ ζωήν. ⟨καὶ⟩ καθ' ὅσον μὲν δίδωσιν ἑαυτὴν εἰς τὰ γιγνόμενα καὶ ὑπὸ τὴν
τοῦ παντὸς φορὰν ἑαυτὴν ὑποτάττει, κατὰ τοσοῦτον καὶ ὑπὸ τὴν εἱμαρμένην
ἄγεται καὶ δουλεύει ταῖς τῆς φύσεως ἀνάγκαις· καθ' ὅσον δὲ αὖ τὴν νοερὰν
ἑαυτῆς καὶ τῷ ὄντι ἄφετον ἀπὸ πάντων καὶ αὐθαίρετον ἐνέργειαν ἐνεργεῖ,
κατὰ τοσοῦτον τὰ ἑαυτῆς ἑκουσίως πράττει καὶ τοῦ θείου καὶ ἀγαθοῦ καὶ
νοητοῦ μετ' ἀληθείας ἐφάπτεται.

3 αὐτή P ‖ 5 καί ante καθ' add. Meineke ‖ 7 αὐτήν F P: αὖ τήν Meineke

Fragment 3
Stobaeus, *Anth.* 2.8.44
2:173,19-24 Wachsmuth

Τὸν κατὰ νοῦν ἄρα βίον καὶ τὸν ἐχόμενον τῶν θεῶν διαζῆν μελετητέον·
οὗτος γὰρ ἡμῖν μόνος ἀποδίδωσι τὴν ἀδέσποτον τῆς ψυχῆς ἐξουσίαν, ἀπολύει
τε ἡμᾶς τῶν ἀναγκαίων δεσμῶν καὶ ποιεῖ ζῆν οὐκ ἀνθρώπινόν τινα βίον,
ἀλλὰ τὸν θεῖον καὶ τῇ βουλήσει τῶν ⟨θεῶν⟩ θείων ἀγαθῶν ἀποπληρούμενον.

1 θείων malit Meineke ‖ 3 ἀναγκαίων F P: ἀνάγκης Heeren; praestat, opinatur Wachsmuth, ἀναγκῶν coll. Iambl. de myst. p. 192, 3 et 208, 1 Parth.
‖ 4 τῶν θείων F P: τῶν θεῶν Wachsmuth, τῶν ⟨θεῶν⟩ θείων Meineke

Fragment 4
Stobaeus, *Anth.* 2.8.45
2:173,26-174,27 Wachsmuth

Καὶ γὰρ ἤδη τὸ ὅλον εἰπεῖν, αἱ μὲν κινήσεις αἱ περὶ τὸν κόσμον
τῆς πεπρωμένης πρὸς τὰς ἀΰλους καὶ νοερὰς ἐνεργείας καὶ περιφορὰς
ἀφομοιοῦνται, ἡ δὲ τάξις αὐτῆς πρὸς τὴν νοητὴν καὶ ἄχραντον εὐταξίαν
ἀπείκασται· τὰ δ' αἴτια τὰ δεύτερα τοῖς προηγουμένοις αἰτίοις συνήρτηται
καὶ τὸ ἐν γενέσει πλῆθος πρὸς τὴν ἀμέριστον οὐσίαν καὶ πάντα οὕτω τὰ
τῆς εἱμαρμένης συνῆπται πρὸς τὴν προηγουμένην πρόνοιαν. κατ' αὐτὴν τὴν
οὐσίαν ἄρα ἐπιπλέκεται ἡ εἱμαρμένη τῇ προνοίᾳ καὶ τῷ εἶναι τὴν πρόνοιάν
ἐστιν ἡ εἱμαρμένη καὶ ἀπ' αὐτῆς καὶ περὶ αὐτὴν ὑφέστηκε.
Τούτων δὲ οὕτως ἐχόντων καὶ ἡ τῶν ἀνθρώπων ἀρχὴ τοῦ πράττειν ἔχει
μὲν συμφωνίαν πρὸς ἀμφοτέρας ταύτας τὰς τοῦ παντὸς ἀρχάς· ἔστι δὲ
καὶ ἀφειμένη ἀπὸ τῆς φύσεως καὶ ἀπόλυτος ἀπὸ τῆς τοῦ παντὸς κινήσεως

tains within itself free and independent life. And in so far as it gives itself to the realm of generation and subjects itself to the flow of the universe, thus far also it is drawn beneath the sway of Fate and is enslaved to the necessities of nature; but in so far, on the other hand, as it exercises its intellectual activity, activity that is really left free from everything and independent in its choices, thus far it voluntarily "minds its own business" and lays hold of what is divine and good and intelligible with the accompaniment of truth.

Fragment 3
It is, then, the life lived in accordance with intellect and that cleaves to the gods that we must train ourselves to live; for this is the only life that admits of the untrammeled authority of the soul, frees us from the bonds of necessity, and allows us to live a life no longer mortal but one that is divine and filled by the will of the gods with divine benefits.

Fragment 4
For indeed, to speak generally, the movements of destiny around the cosmos are assimilated to the immaterial and intellectual activities and circuits, and its order is assimilated to the good order of the intelligible and transcendent realm. And the secondary causes are dependent on the primary causes, and the multiplicity attendant upon generation on the undivided substance, and the whole sum of things subject to Fate is thus connected to the dominance of Providence. In its very substance, then, Fate is enmeshed with Providence, and Fate exists by virtue of the existence of Providence, and it derives its existence from it and within its ambit.
This being the case, then, the originating cause of action in humans has indeed a concordance with both these originating causes in the universe; but it is also the case that the origin of action in us is both independent of Nature and emancipated from the movement of the uni-

⟨ἡ⟩ ἐν ἡμῖν τῶν πράξεων ἀρχή. διὰ τοῦτο οὐκ ἔνεστιν ἐν τῇ τοῦ παντός. διότι μὲν γὰρ ⟨οὐκ⟩ ἀπὸ τῆς φύσεως παράγεται οὐδὲ ἀπὸ τῆς τοῦ παντὸς κινήσεως, πρεσβυτέρα καὶ οὐκ ἀπὸ τοῦ παντὸς ἐνδιδομένη, προτέτακται·
15 διότι γε μὴν ἀφ' ὅλων τῶν τοῦ κόσμου μερίδων καὶ ἀπὸ πάντων στοιχείων μοίρας τινὰς κατενείματο καὶ ταύταις πάσαις χρῆται, περιέχεται αὐτὴ καὶ ἐν τῇ τῆς εἱμαρμένης διατάξει, συντελεῖ τε εἰς αὐτὴν καὶ συμπληροῖ τὴν ἐν αὐτῇ κατασκευὴν καὶ χρῆται αὐτῇ δεόντως. καὶ καθ' ὅσον μὲν λόγον καθαρὸν αὐθυπόστατον καὶ αὐτοκίνητον ἀφ' ἑαυτοῦ τε ἐνεργοῦντα καὶ
20 τέλειον ἡ ψυχὴ συνείληφεν ἐν ἑαυτῇ, κατὰ τοσοῦτον ἀπόλυτός ἐστι πάντων τῶν ἔξωθεν· καθ' ὅσον γε μὴν καὶ ζωὰς ἄλλας προβάλλει ῥεπούσας εἰς τὴν γένεσιν καὶ ἐπικοινωνεῖ τῷ σώματι, κατὰ τοσοῦτον ἔχει συμπλοκὴν καὶ πρὸς τὴν τοῦ κόσμου διάταξιν.

5 πρὸς scripsit Wachsmuth pro περί || 8 post ὑφέστηκε clausula significata est in F P || 10–11 ἔστι δὲ καὶ ἀφειμένη scripsit Wachsmuth pro ἔχει δὲ καὶ ἀφειμένην || 11–12 ἀπόλυτος et ἀρχή scripsit Wachsmuth pro ἀπόλυτον et ἀρχήν || 12 ἡ add. Dillon || 13 οὐκ add. Wachsmuth || 16 περιέχει ταύτῃ F P: corr. Heeren || 17 συντελεῖται F P: συντελεῖ τε Meineke, Wachsmuth: καὶ συντελεῖται Heeren || 19 ἀνυπόστατον P || 20 καὶ τοσοῦτον P || 22 τὸ σῶμα F P: corr. Heeren | καὶ τοσοῦτον P

Fragment 5
Stobaeus, Anth. 2.8.46
2:175,2–15 Wachsmuth

Εἰ δέ τις ταὐτόματον καὶ τὴν τύχην ἐπεισάγων ἀναιρεῖν οἴεται τὴν τάξιν, μαθέτω ὡς οὐδέν ἐστιν ἐν τῷ παντὶ ἄτακτον οὐδ' ἐπεισοδιῶδες οὐδὲ ἄνευ αἰτίας οὐδ' ἀόριστον οὐδὲ εἰκῇ οὐδ' ἀπὸ τοῦ μηδενὸς ἐπεισιὸν οὐδὲ κατὰ συμβεβηκός. οὔκουν ἀναιρεῖται ἡ τάξις καὶ συνέχεια τῶν αἰτιῶν καὶ ἡ τῶν
5 ἀρχῶν ἕνωσις καὶ ἡ δι' ὅλων διατείνουσα τῶν πρώτων ἐπικράτεια. βέλτιον οὖν ἀφορίζεσθαι· ἡ τύχη τῶν πλειόνων τάξεων ἢ καὶ ἄλλων δή τινων [ἢ] ἔστιν ἔφορος καὶ συναγωγὸς αἰτία, πρεσβυτέρα τῶν συνιόντων, ἣν τότε μὲν θεὸν ἐπικαλοῦμεν, ⟨τότε δὲ δαίμονα⟩ παρειλήφαμεν. ἡνίκα μὲν γὰρ ἂν τὰ κρείττονα αἴτια τῶν συν⟨ιόντων⟩ ᾖ, θεός ἐστιν αὐτῶν ἔφορος, ὁπόταν δὲ τὰ
10 ἐν τῇ φύσει, δαίμων. ἀεὶ οὖν μετ' αἰτίας πάντα ἐπιτελεῖται καὶ οὐδ' ὁτιοῦν ἄτακτον ἐν τοῖς γιγνομένοις ἐπεισέρχεται.

1 ψυχήν F P: corr. Canter || 6 ἢ secl. Meineke || 8 ἢν παρελείφαμεν F P: τότε δὲ δαίμονα παρειλήφαμεν Heeren cum Cantero || 9 συνι Ἡ (spat. 2

verse. For this reason it is not implicated in the originative principle of the universe. For because it is not produced from Nature, nor produced from the movement of the universe, it is ranked above it as prior, and not dependent on the universe; but because it has taken for itself portions from all the parts of the cosmos and from all of the elements and makes use of all these, it is itself also included in the order of Fate, and contributes to it, and assists in the fulfillment of its constitution, and is necessarily involved with it. And in so far as the soul contains within itself a pure, self-subsistent, self-motive, active and perfective reason-principle, thus far it is emancipated from all outside influences; but on the other hand, insofar as it puts forth other levels of life that incline toward generation and consort with the body, thus far it is involved in the order of the cosmos.

Fragment 5

But if anyone, by dragging in the spontaneous and Chance, thinks to abolish the order (of the cosmos), let him realize that nothing in the universe is unordered nor adventitious nor devoid of cause nor undefined nor random nor arising from nothing nor yet accidental. There is no question, therefore, of abolishing order and continuity of causes and the unity of first principles and the domination of the primal essences extending throughout everything. It is better, then, to make a definition as follows: Chance is the overseer and connecting cause of a plurality of orders of events or of whatever else, being superior to what comes together under it, an entity that we sometimes denominate a god and sometimes take as being a daemon. For whenever the higher beings are causes of events, a god is their overseer, while when it is natural forces that are the causes, it is a daemon (sc. that presides). All things therefore always come to fruition in conjunction with a cause, and nothing at all unordered obtrudes itself into the realm of becoming.

litt.) F, συνϊ H (spat. 5 litt.) P: συνιόντων ᾖ cum Heereno Meineke, qui add. "fortasse tamen praestat αἴτια ᾖ ὧν συνίῃ" ‖ **10** δαιμόνων P

Fragment 6
Stobaeus, *Anth.* 2.8.47
2:175,17–176,10 Wachsmuth

   Διὰ τί οὖν παρ' ἀξίαν αἱ διανομαὶ ἀποδίδονται; ἢ τοῦτο οὐδὲ τὴν ἀρχὴν ἀμφισβητεῖν ὅσιον; οὐ γὰρ ἐπ' ἄλλῳ τινὶ κεῖται, ἐπ' αὐτῷ δὲ τῷ ἀνθρώπῳ καὶ τῇ τοῦ ἀνθρώπου αἱρέσει τἀγαθά, καὶ ταῦτα ἐν τῇ προαιρέσει μόνον κυριώτατα δὴ ἀφώρισται, τὰ δὲ ἀπορούμενα παρὰ τοῖς πολλοῖς δι' ἄγνοιαν
5 ἀμφισβητεῖται. οὐκ ἄλλη οὖν ἐπικαρπία τῆς ἀρετῆς ἐστιν ἢ αὐτὴ ἑαυτῆς. οὐ μὴν οὐδὲ ἐλαττοῦται ὅστις σπουδαῖος ἀπὸ τῆς τύχης, κρείττονα γὰρ αὐτὸν πάσης συντυχίας ἡ μεγαλοψυχία ἀπεργάζεται. οὐδὲ γὰρ παρὰ φύσιν γίγνεται· ἐξαρκεῖ γὰρ ἡ τῆς ψυχῆς ἀκρότης καὶ τελειότης τὴν ἀρίστην φύσιν συμπληρῶσαι τοῦ ἀνθρώπου. καὶ μὴν τά γε ἐναντία εἶναι δοκοῦντα γυμνάζει
10 καὶ συνέχει καὶ συναύξει τὴν ἀρετὴν καὶ οὐχ οἷόν ἐστι χωρὶς αὐτῶν καλοὺς κἀγαθοὺς γίγνεσθαι. καὶ αὕτη τοίνυν ἡ διάθεσις τοῦ σπουδαίου τὸ καλὸν προτιμᾷ τε διαφερόντως καὶ τὴν τοῦ λόγου τελειότητα μόνην ἐν μακαρίᾳ ζωῇ τίθεται, τὰ δὲ ἄλλα ἐν οὐδενὸς μέρει περιορᾷ καὶ ἀτιμάζει.

Fragment 7
Stobaeus, *Anth.* 2.8.48
2:176,12–21 Wachsmuth

   Ἐπεὶ τοίνυν ἐν ψυχῇ μέν ἐστιν ὁ ἄνθρωπος, ἡ δὲ ψυχὴ νοερά τε ἐστὶ καὶ ἀθάνατος, καὶ τὸ καλὸν ἄρα αὐτῆς καὶ τὸ ἀγαθὸν καὶ τὸ τέλος ἐνυπάρχει τῇ θείᾳ ζωῇ, τῶν δὲ θνητοειδῶν οὐδὲν κύριον ἢ συμβάλλεσθαί τι πρὸς τὴν τελείαν ζωήν ἐστιν, ἢ παραιρεῖν αὐτῆς τὴν εὐδαιμονίαν. ὅλως γὰρ ἐν
5 νοερᾷ μὲν ζωῇ τὸ μακάριον ἡμῖν ὑπάρχει· ταύτην δὲ οὐδὲν τῶν μέσων οὔτε ἐπιδιδόναι ποιεῖ οὔτ' ἐστὶν ἀφαιρεῖσθαι. Μάτην ἄρα αἱ τύχαι καὶ τὰ ἄνισα δῶρα τῆς τύχης διατεθρύληται παρὰ τοῖς ἀνθρώποις.

3 δέ F, τε P

Fragment 6

Why, then, are deserts apportioned undeservedly? Or is it not even proper to raise this question? For benefits are not dependent on any external cause but on the individual himself and on his free choice, and these are most properly defined in connection with one's chosen mode of life, and the problems raised by the majority of men arise out of ignorance. There is, then, no fruit of virtue other than virtue itself. This is not to say that the good man is worsted by Chance, for his greatness of spirit renders him superior to all accidents of fortune. Nor, I may add, does this come about contrary to nature; for the summit and perfection of the soul is sufficient to fulfill the best nature of man. And indeed what seem to be reverses in fact serve to exercise and coordinate and stimulate virtue, and it is not possible without them to develop a noble character. This state of mind of the good man gives particular honor to nobility and regards only the complete fulfillment of reason as constituting the happy life, while ignoring and despising as of no worth everything else.

Fragment 7

So then, since man's true essence lies in his soul, and the soul is intelligent and immortal, and its nobility and its good and its end reposes in divine life, nothing of mortal nature has power to contribute anything toward the perfect life or to deprive it of happiness. For in general our blessedness resides in intellectual life; for none of the median things has the capacity either to increase or to nullify it. It is therefore irrelevant to go on, as men generally do, about Chance and its unequal gifts.

Letter 9
Πρὸς Μακεδόνιον περὶ ὁμονοίας

Stobaeus, *Anth.* 2.33.15
2:257,5-17 Wachsmuth

Ἡ ὁμόνοια, καθάπερ αὐτὸ τὸ ὄνομα βούλεται ἐνδείκνυσθαι, συναγωγὴν ὁμοίου τοῦ νοῦ κοινωνίαν τε καὶ ἕνωσιν ἐν ἑαυτῇ συνείληφεν· ἀφορμηθεῖσα δὴ οὖν ἐντεῦθεν ἐπὶ πόλεις καὶ οἴκους, κοινούς τε συλλόγους πάντας καὶ ἰδίους [οἴκους], φύσεις τε καὶ συγγενείας πάσας ἐπιπορεύεται, κοινάς τε καὶ ἰδίας
5 ὡσαύτως· ἔτι δὲ περιέχει καὶ τὴν ἑνὸς ἑκάστου πρὸς ἑαυτὸν ὁμογνωμοσύνην· ὑφ' ἑνὸς μὲν γάρ τις νοήματος καὶ μιᾶς γνώμης κυβερνώμενος ὁμονοεῖ πρὸς ἑαυτόν, διχογνωμονῶν δὲ πρὸς ἑαυτὸν καὶ ἀνόμοια λογιζόμενος διαστασιάζει· καὶ ὁ μὲν ἐπὶ τῆς ἀεὶ αὐτῆς ἐπιμένων διανοήσεως ὁμοφροσύνης ἐστὶ πλήρης· ὁ δὲ ἄστατος τοῖς λογισμοῖς καὶ ἄλλοτε ἐπ' ἄλλην δόξην φερόμενος
10 ἀστάθμητός ἐστι καὶ πολέμιος πρὸς ἑαυτόν.

---

2 ὃ μόνον L: ὁμοίου Halm lect. Stob. p. 59, ὁμοῦ Gaisford || 4 οἴκους secl. Meineke in praef. (minus recte in textu scripsit ἤκουσα) || 9 ἐπ' ἄλλης δόξης L: ἐπ' ἄλλην δόξην Wachsmuth, ὑπ' ἄλλης δόξης Halm, ἀπ' ἄλλης δόξης Meineke

Letter 9
To Macedonius, On Concord

Concord, even as the name itself suggests, involves a communion and unity that brings together kindred minds; starting out from this base, it extends itself to cities and homes, to all gatherings public and private, and to all natures and kinship-groups, public and private likewise. And further, it comprehends also the concordance of each individual with himself; for it is by being governed by a single mindset and attitude that a man is concordant with himself, while if he is in two minds toward himself and holds variant opinions, he is in conflict with himself. The former, always remaining in the same state of mind, is full of concord, whereas the latter, being unstable in his views and liable to be driven from one opinion to another, is lacking in solid foundation and at war with himself.

Letter 10
Πρὸς Ὀλύμπιον περὶ ἀνδρείας

Fragment 1
Stobaeus, *Anth.* 3.7.40
3:319,21–320,5 Hense

Ἀνδρεία νοείσθω ἡ κυριωτάτη, ὅση τέ ἐστιν ἄτρεπτος νοερὰ δύναμις, καὶ ὅση ἀκμαιοτάτη νοερὰ ἐνέργεια, ἥτε τοῦ νοῦ ταυτότης καὶ μόνιμος ἕξις ἐν ἑαυτῇ· τοιαῦτα ἂν εἴη τὰ περὶ τὴν ζωὴν εἴδη θεωρούμενα τῆς ἀνδρείας, ἤτοι καθ᾽ ἑαυτὰ ὑφεστηκότα ἢ κοινωνήσαντα τὴν ἑαυτῶν ῥώμην πρὸς τὴν ἐν τοῖς
5   λόγοις μόνιμον κατάστασιν.

Fragment 2
Stobaeus, *Anth.* 3.7.41
3:320,7–21 Hense

Ἀπὸ δὴ τούτων τὰ ἐν τοῖς πάθεσιν περί τε δεινὰ καὶ μὴ δεινὰ καὶ περὶ φόβον καὶ θάρσος περί τε ἡδονὴν καὶ λύπην γενναίως ἀνθιστάμενα, καὶ τὰ διαφυλάττοντα ἀεὶ τὰς αὐτὰς ὀρθὰς δόξας, τά τε σύμμετρα καὶ μέσα ἤδη διασῴζοντα, καὶ τὰ πραΰνοντα τὸν <θυμὸν> ὑπὸ τῷ λόγῳ καὶ
5   ἀνεγείροντα αὐτὸν κατὰ καιρόν, καὶ τὰ κοινὰ τούτων ἐκ πάθους καὶ λόγου καὶ προαιρέσεως, τίθεμαι εἶναι πολυμέριστα εἴδη τῆς ἀνδρείας· ἀφ᾽ ὧν ἐπιρρεῖ τοῖς βίοις ἡ ἀνδραγαθία τῶν πράξεων ἀήττητος πάντῃ καὶ ἀβίαστος, ἑκουσίως τὰ καλὰ καὶ δι᾽ ἑαυτὰ αἱρουμένη καὶ πράττουσα, καὶ τῶν ἀγαθῶν ἕνεκα πάντας πόνους καὶ κινδύνους ὑπομένουσα διδοῦσά τε ἑαυτὴν ἑτοίμως
10 εἰς τὰ δοκοῦντα εἶναι δυσχερῆ, καὶ θαρροῦσα τὸν θάνατον καὶ μελετῶσα τάς τε ἀλγηδόνας εὐκόλως φέρουσα καὶ μεταχειριζομένη.

---

4 τὸν θυμὸν τῷ λ. ci. Wachsmuth ‖ **6** εἴδη ex ἤθη fecit A¹: ἤθη Mᵈ, inde Gesn.², vulg. sed εἴδη ci. Gesn.² p. 89 mrg

Letter 10
To Olympius, On Courage

Fragment 1
Let courage in the most proper sense be understood to be such as is an unshakable intellectual potency, and the highest form of intellectual activity, and which constitutes self-identity of intellect and a state of mind steadfast within itself; such would be the manifestations of courage as viewed in the course of daily life, either as established on their own or as combining their strength with a steadfast attitude in one's reasonings.

Fragment 2
From these, then, derive those forces that, in the realm of the passions, take a noble stand in relation to what is and what is not to be feared, and in relation to fear itself and boldness, and in relation to pleasure and pain, and which preserve always the same correct opinions, and keep to the harmonious and median path, and both calm <the spirit> under the influence of reason and in turn rouse it up when the need arises, and establish a common purpose for these compounded out of passion and reason and will, these I hold to be the various forms of courage. And from these there flows into people's lives a nobility of action that is thoroughly indefeasible and unconquerable, willingly choosing and performing noble deeds for their own sake, and in the cause of the good undergoing every sort of toil and danger, devoting itself readily to tasks that seem difficult, maintaining good cheer in the face of death, and indeed practicing it, while bearing and dealing with pains with equanimity.

Letter 11
Πρὸς Ποιμένιον περὶ εἱμαρμένης (?)

Stobaeus, *Anth.* 1.1.35
1:43,2–14 Wachsmuth

Οἱ θεοὶ τὴν εἱμαρμένην συνέχοντες διὰ παντὸς ἐπανορθοῦνται· ἡ δ' ἐπανόρθωσις αὐτῶν ποτὲ μὲν ἐλάττωσιν κακῶν, ποτὲ δὲ παραμυθίαν, ἐνίοτε δὲ καὶ ἀναίρεσιν ἀπεργάζεται· ἀφ' οὗ δὴ διακοσμεῖται ἡ εἱμαρμένη τοῖς ἀγαθοῖς, διακοσμουμένη δὲ οὐχ ὑποφαίνεται πᾶσα πρὸς τὴν ἄτακτον φύσιν
5 τῆς γενέσεως. οὐκοῦν ἔτι μᾶλλον σώζεται ἡ πεπρωμένη διὰ τῆς τοιαύτης ἐπανορθώσεως καὶ τὸ παρατρέπον αὐτῆς μένει κατὰ τὴν ἄτρεπτον τῶν θεῶν ἀγαθότητα συνεχόμενον, διότι οὐκ ἐᾶται ὑπορρεῖν εἰς τὴν ἄτακτον πλημμέλειαν. τούτων δ' οὕτως ἐχόντων τό τε ἀγαθοειδὲς τῆς προνοίας τό τε αὐτεξούσιον τῆς ψυχῆς καὶ πάντα τὰ κάλλιστα διασώζεται, τῇ βουλήσει
10 τῶν θεῶν συνυπάρχοντα.

Letter 11
To Poemenius, On Fate (?)

The gods, in upholding fate, direct its operation throughout the universe, and this sound direction of theirs brings about sometimes a lessening of evils, sometimes a mitigation of their effects, on occasion even their removal. On this principle, then, Fate is disposed to the benefit of the good but in this disposing does not reveal itself fully to the disorderly nature of the realm of generation. So then, even more so is destiny preserved by means of such sound direction, and that aspect of it that is perverted remains comprehended by the unalterable goodness of the gods, since this does not permit it to dissolve into disorderly error. This being the case, both the goodness of providence and the freedom of choice of the soul and all the best elements of reality are vindicated, kept in being together by the will of the gods.

Letter 12
Πρὸς Σώπατρον περὶ εἱμαρμένης

Stobaeus, Anth. 1.5.18
1:81,8–18 Wachsmuth

Τῆς δ' εἱμαρμένης ἡ οὐσία σύμπασά ἐστιν ἐν τῇ φύσει· φύσιν δὲ λέγω τὴν ἀχώριστον αἰτίαν τοῦ κόσμου καὶ ἀχωρίστως περιέχουσαν τὰς ὅλας αἰτίας τῆς γενέσεως, ὅσα χωριστῶς αἱ κρείττονες οὐσίαι καὶ διακοσμήσεις συνειλήφασιν ἐν ἑαυταῖς. ζωή τε οὖν σωματοειδὴς καὶ λόγος γενεσιουργός,
5 τά τε ἔνυλα εἴδη καὶ αὐτὴ ἡ ὕλη, ἥ τε συντεθειμένη γένεσις ἀπὸ τούτων, κίνησίς τε ἡ τὰ πάντα μεταβάλλουσα καὶ φύσις ἡ τεταγμένως διοικοῦσα τὰ γιγνόμενα, ἀρχαί τε αἱ τῆς φύσεως καὶ τέλη καὶ ποιήσεις, καὶ αἱ τούτων συνδέσεις πρὸς ἄλληλα ἀπ' ἀρχῆς τε ἄχρι τοῦ τέλους διέξοδοι συμπληροῦσι τὴν εἱμαρμένην.

---

3 ὅσα F P¹ Wachsmuth, ὅσας P² || 7 ποίησις FP: corr. Heeren

Letter 12
To Sopater, On Fate

The essence of Fate subsists entirely within the ambit of Nature, by which latter I mean the immanent causal principle of the cosmos and that which immanently comprises the totality of causes of the realm of generation, such as the higher essences and orders comprehend within themselves in a transcendent mode. That life, therefore, which relates to body and the rational principle which is concerned with generation, the forms-in-matter and Matter itself, and the creation that is put together out of these elements, and that motion which produces change in all of these, and that Nature which administers in an orderly way all things that come into being, and the beginnings and ends and creations of Nature, and the combinations of these with each other and their progressions from beginning to end—all these go to make up the essence of Fate.

Letter 13
Πρὸς Σώπατρον περὶ διαλεκτικῆς

Fragment 1
Stobaeus, *Anth.* 2.2.6
2:19,14–20,16 Wachsmuth

Πάντες ἄνθρωποι χρῶνται τῷ διαλέγεσθαι, ἔμφυτον ἐκ νέων ἔχοντες τήνδε τὴν δύναμιν καὶ μέχρι τινός, οἳ μὲν μᾶλλον οἳ δὲ ἧττον αὐτῆς μετέχοντες. τὸ δὴ τῶν θεῶν δῶρον οὐδένα τρόπον δεῖ προΐεσθαι· ἀλλὰ καὶ ἐν μελέταις καὶ ἐμπειρίαις καὶ τέχναις αὐτὸ κρατύνειν ἄξιον. ὅρα γὰρ ὅτι
5 καὶ παρ' ὅλον τὸν βίον διατελεῖ χρησιμώτατον ὂν διαφερόντως, ἐν μὲν ταῖς ἐντεύξεσι προσομιλοῦν τοῖς ἀνθρώποις κατὰ τὰς κοινὰς ἐννοίας καὶ δόξας· ἐν δὲ ταῖς εὑρέσεσι τῶν τεχνῶν τὰς πρώτας ἀρχὰς αὐτῶν ἀνευρίσκον· λογιζόμενον δὲ πρὸ τῶν ἔργων, ὅπως αὐτὰ χρὴ πράττειν· προγυμνασίᾳ δὲ καὶ πρὸς τὰς κατὰ φιλοσοφίαν ἐπιστήμας θαυμασίας οἵας μεθόδους
10 παρεχόμενον. εἰ δὲ δεῖ καὶ τὰ πρὸ τούτων ἐννοεῖν, οὐκ ἔστιν οὐδὲν μόριον φιλοσοφίας ἄνευ τοῦ κατὰ διαλεκτικὴν λόγου παραγιγνόμενον· ἀλλὰ καὶ εἴ τι φυσικὸν δόγμα ἀνευρίσκομεν, λογικῶς αὐτὸ βεβαιούμεθα, καὶ ὅσα περὶ θεῶν σκεπτόμεθα, λόγος διαλεκτικός ἐστιν ὁ συγκατασκευάσας· ὅλως δὲ οὐδὲν οὔτε εἰπεῖν οὔτε ἀκοῦσαι δυνατὸν ἀπαλλαγέντας τῆς μεθόδου ταύτης·
15 καὶ γὰρ αὐτὸ τὸ μὴ διδάσκειν διαλεκτικὴν διαλεκτικῶς ἐπιχειροῦντας δεῖ καταμανθάνειν. εἴτε οὖν ἐπιτηδευτέον, εἴτε μή, διαλεκτικὴν ἀσκεῖν ⟨ἄξιον⟩· καὶ γάρ ἐστιν ἄτοπον, εἰ τὰ μὲν ἅπαντα λόγῳ κρίνομεν, αὐτὴν ⟨δὲ⟩ ἀφήσομεν τὴν ἀκριβεστάτην τοῦ λόγου θεωρίαν· καὶ λόγῳ προέχοντες τῶν ἄλλων ζῴων καὶ τοῦτο ἐξαίρετον ἀγαθὸν κεκτημένοι τῆς ἀνθρωπίνης φύσεως, εἰκῇ καὶ ὡς
20 ἔτυχε τὰ κατ' αὐτὸν ἐνεργήσομεν· καὶ τὴν συμμεμιγμένην διάσκεψιν τοῦ λόγου πρὸς τὰ ὅλα πράγματα ἀγαπῶμεν, αὐτὴν δὲ τὴν ἑαυτοῦ γνῶσιν τοῦ λόγου, καθ' ἣν ἀφέμενος τῶν ἄλλων τὴν περὶ αὐτοῦ ἐπιστήμην κατεστήσατο σεμνοτάτην οὖσαν καὶ τιμιωτάτην, ὡς μαρτυρεῖ καὶ τὸ ἐν Πυθοῖ γράμμα, ἀποδοκιμάσομεν ὡς ἀπόβλητον.

---

16 ἄξιον add. Hense || **17** μὲν ἄλλα πάντα vulg.: μὲν ἅπαντα Wachsmuth | δὲ om. ABS: add. vulg. || **22** αὐτοῦ corr. Meineke

Letter 13
To Sopater, On Dialectic

Fragment 1

All men employ dialectic, since this power is innate in them from their earliest years, at least to some degree, though some have a larger share of it than others. Something that is a gift of the gods should by no means be cast aside but should rather be fortified by practice and experience and technical training. For behold how during one's whole life it continues to be outstandingly useful: in one's encounters with one's fellow-men, for addressing them in accordance with the common notions and opinions; in investigations in the arts and sciences, for discovering the first principles of each; for calculating, prior to each action, how one should proceed; and for providing marvelous methods of preliminary training for the various philosophical sciences.

And if we are to focus on more basic questions, there is no part of philosophy that comes into being without the aid of dialectical argument: even if we discover some theory in the natural sciences, we confirm it with the aid of logic; and if we are speculating about the gods, it is a dialectical argument that gives us the basis for that. And in general, it is not possible either to utter or to take in any proposition if we dispense with this method of procedure; indeed, the very decision not to teach dialectic must be arrived at through the practice of dialectic.

So then, whether it is to be practiced or not, in either case we must arrive at the decision through dialectic, and indeed it is absurd if we judge all other things by the use of reasoning but dispense with just that method that constitutes the most accurate study of reasoning. And again, though it is by virtue of reason that we are superior to other animals, and have acquired this as a distinctive benefit of human nature, are we then to exercise the activities associated with it in a random and careless manner? Again, shall we accept reason's composite study of the whole of reality but dismiss as dispensable reason's knowledge of itself, in virtue of which it turns aside from everything else and has established the scientific study of itself, the most serious and honorable science of all, as indeed is testified to by the inscription in Delphi?

Fragment 2
Stobaeus, *Anth.* 2.2.7
2:20,18–21,14 Wachsmuth

Μετίωμεν δὴ οὖν ἐπὶ τὰς κατὰ φιλοσοφίαν διατριβάς. Πασῶν πρῶταί εἰσιν αἱ πρὸς ἀνάμνησιν ἀναγόμεναι· ταύτας δὴ οὖν, <ὥς> καὶ ὁ Σωκράτης ἐπιδεικνύει ἐν τῷ Μένωνι, διὰ τοῦ καλῶς ἐρωτᾶν ὁρῶμεν ἐκφαινομένας. Δεύτεραι δ' ἂν εἶεν αἱ μαιείας ἕνεκα προσαγόμεναι καὶ τὰ γεννηθέντα εἰς
5 φῶς προάγουσαι καὶ διακρίνουσαι τίνα μὲν αὐτῶν ἀληθῆ, τίνα δὲ ψευδῆ. ἀλλὰ καὶ αὗται πᾶσαι διὰ τῆς διαλεκτικῆς τὸ κῦρος ἔχουσιν· ἐπειδὴ αὗταί εἰσιν αἱ διὰ τῶν ἐλέγχων καθάρσεις τῆς διανοίας, παρατιθεῖσαι τἀναντία δοξάσματα τῶν προσδιαλεγομένων καὶ συγκρούουσαι αὐτὰ πρὸς ἄλληλα. ἄλλαι δὲ πείρας ἕνεκα καὶ γυμνασίας προσφερόμεναι τοῖς ἐπηκόοις, ἢ ὅσαι
10 εἰς θέσιν ἐπιχειροῦσιν, ἢ εἴ τινες ἐξετάζουσι τὰς τῶν παλαιῶν ἀκροάσεις· ὧν οὐδεμία ⟨δίχα⟩ διαλεκτικῆς περαίνει τὸ ἑαυτῆς ἔργον. ὅλως δὲ οὐχ οἷόν τε λόγον διδόναι καὶ λαμβάνειν δεόντως, εἰ μή τις κτήσαιτο ταύτην τὴν περὶ τὸν λόγον ἐπιστήμην.

---

2 ὥς add. Wachsmuth || 11 δίχα add. Wachsmuth

Fragment 2

Let us turn, then, to the activities associated with philosophy. Primary among all are those that conduce to recollection. These, as indeed Socrates demonstrates in the *Meno*, we see illustrated through good techniques of questioning. Second would be those that are engaged in for the purpose of "midwifery," bringing the products of the process to light and distinguishing which of them are true and which false. But all these derive their validity from dialectic, since these are the purifications of the intellect through refutations, juxtaposing opposite opinions for those engaged in disputation and testing them against each other. And others are presented to the auditors for the sake of testing and exercise, either such as advance a thesis or if there are some that test the doctrines of the ancients; of these none achieves its purpose without dialectic. And in general it is not possible to give or receive a rational account in due order, unless one has acquired this science of rational argument.

Letter 14
Πρὸς Σώπατρον περὶ παίδων ἀγωγῆς

Stobaeus, *Anth.* 2.31.122
2:233,19–235,22 Wachsmuth

 Παντὸς ζῴου καὶ φυτοῦ ἡ πρώτη βλάστη καλῶς ὁρμηθεῖσα πρὸς τὴν ἑκάστου ἀρετὴν κυριωτάτη πασῶν ἐστι τέλος ἐπιθεῖναι τὸ πρόσφορον, καὶ τῆς τῶν παίδων τοίνυν εὐεξίας ἡ πρώτη βελτίστη τῆς φύσεως πρόοδος ὁδῷ ⟨τε⟩ πρόεισιν ἐπὶ τὴν τελειότητα τεταγμένως, ἐφ᾽ ἥνπερ αὐτὴν προχωρεῖν
5 ἄξιον· ταύτην τοίνυν ἡ ὀρθὴ παιδεία δεόντως προοδηγεῖ, σπέρματα τῶν ἀρετῶν ἤδη προκαταβαλλομένη καὶ ἐν ἁπαλαῖς ἔτι καὶ ἀβάτοις ψυχαῖς θαυμαστὴν οἰκείωσιν ἐμποιοῦσα πρὸς τὴν τῶν καλῶν ἐπιτήδευσιν. πρῶτον μὲν οὖν διὰ τῶν αἰσθήσεων ἐν πατρὶ καὶ μητρὶ καὶ παιδαγωγῷ καὶ διδασκάλῳ προτείνει παραδείγματα τῶν καλῶν ἔργων, ἵνα οἱ θεώμενοι
10 παῖδες αὐτὰ ζηλῶσιν τὴν πρὸς αὐτοὺς ἀφομοίωσιν· ἔπειτα τοῖς ἔθεσιν ἄγει καλῶς καὶ ἐμποιεῖ τὰ σπουδαῖα ἤθη, μήπω δυναμένων αὐτῶν λόγῳ λαμβάνειν, διά [τε] τῆς συνηθείας τῶν καλῶν τρέπουσα αὐτῶν τὰς ψυχὰς πρὸς τὸ βέλτιον, ἐπὶ δὲ τούτοις συμφωνίαν ἡδονῆς καὶ λύπης πρὸς τὰ καλὰ ⟨καὶ αἰσχρὰ⟩ ἔργα παρασκευάζει, ὥστε μὴ μόνον πράττειν τὰ καλὰ
15 ἔργα, ἀλλὰ καὶ χαίρειν ἐπ᾽ αὐτοῖς συμμέτρως, μηδὲ ἀποφεύγειν μόνον τὰ αἰσχρά, ἀλλὰ καὶ δυσχεραίνειν αὐτὰ ἐγκαιρότατα· προάγουσιν δὲ αὐτοῖς ἐνταῦθα, ὃ χρὴ προηγεῖσθαι παντὸς [τοῦ] ὀρθοῦ βίου, τὴν ἐπὶ τοῖς αἰσχροῖς αἰσχύνην καὶ ἐπὶ τοῖς καλοῖς φιλοτιμίαν ἐντίθησι, δι᾽ ὧν ἀπάγονται μὲν πάντων τῶν αἰσχρῶν καὶ εὐλάβειάν τινα πρὸς αὐτὰ κτῶνται, ἐφίενται δὲ
20 τῶν ἀγαθῶν καὶ πρὸς αὐτὰ σύντονον ὁρμὴν προσλαμβάνουσι· μετὰ δὲ ταῦτα προστάγματά τινα νουθετητικά, μικρὰ μὲν ὄντα τοῖς ῥήμασι, μεγάλην δέ τινα δύναμιν τοῖς τηλικούτοις παρεχόμενα, οἷον τὸ "δεῖ" καί ποτε "οὐ δεῖ" καὶ τὸ "μέχρι πόσου;" καὶ "ποῖόν τι τὸ ἄριστόν ἐστι [μέτρον];" καὶ "τίς τὰ τοιαῦτα;" συμμετρίαν αὐτοῖς ἐναρμόζει τὴν πρὸς ἀλλότριον λόγον
25 συνταττομένην, οἷον τοῦ νομοθέτου καὶ διδασκάλου· καὶ τό γε δὴ κράτιστον

Letter 14
To Sopater, On Bringing Up Children

The initial sprouting of every animal and plant, if it starts off well, is the most powerful factor of all, in relation to the virtue of each, in imposing a fortunate outcome, and in the case of the well-being of children the first progression of nature, if it is the best, proceeds in order and sequence toward that perfection toward which it is proper that it should proceed. It is this, then, to which correct education properly leads, through laying down in advance the seeds of the virtues and instilling in souls still "tender and uncorrupted" a wondrous degree of affinity toward the practice of noble activities.

First of all, through the senses, in the persons of father and mother and tutor and teacher, it sets out models of noble actions, in order that the children, as they behold them, may strive to assimilate themselves to them. Then, by means of training, it leads them on nobly and instills good habits, while they are not yet able to take in a reasoned account, by familiarization with what is noble turning their souls toward the better; and over and above this, it creates a harmony of pleasure and pain in response to noble <and base> actions, so that they should not only perform noble acts but also take proper pleasure in them, and not only shun base actions but also be disgusted at them in the most appropriate manner.

When they have advanced to this point—and this is something that should form the prelude to any rightly organized life—it instills into them shame at what is base and emulation of what is noble, by dint of which they are turned away from all base actions and acquire a certain instinctive distaste for them, while being stimulated toward good actions and acquiring an intense zeal for the achievement of such actions. Indeed, after such admonitory exhortations as these, which may be brief in terms of words but possess great power over anyone trained in this way—such as "You should…" and sometimes "You should not…" and "How far (should you go)?" and "What is the best course of action?" and "What sort of person would do such things?"—it imposes on them a measured mindset that can respond to the argument of another, such as a lawgiver or a teacher. And the most important thing is to be able to

ἔστι τὰ οἰκεῖα παραγγέλματα καὶ νουθετήματα ⟨τὰ⟩ φέροντα πρὸς ἑκάστην ἀρετὴν παραδιδόναι δεόντως, τὰ μὲν ἐν κοιναῖς γνώμαις, τὰ δ' ἐν ἔργων ἀσκήσει, τὰ δ' ἐν τῇ τῶν λόγων μελέτῃ, τὰ δ' ἐν ταῖς ὑποθήκαις περί τῶν πρακτέων ἢ μὴ πρακτέων, τὰ δ' ἐν ταῖς τῆς ζωῆς κατασκευαῖς. ἐπειδὰν δὲ
30 τούτων ἕνεκα ἱκανῶς ἔχωσι, τοῖς λόγοις αὐτοὺς παιδευτέον, ἀρχομένους ἀπὸ τῶν ἁπλουστέρων καὶ γνωριμωτέρων, ἔπειτα προϊόντας ὁσημέραι καὶ κατὰ βραχὺ πρὸς τοὺς τῆς αἰτίας ἀπολογισμούς· καὶ ἐπὶ τούτων τὸ μὲν δι' εὐκρινείας ἐπιστημονικῆς τελέως φυλακτέον ἔτι ἀτελέσι διανοίαις παρακατατίθεσθαι, τὰ δὲ ὡς ἔπος εἰπεῖν ⟨...⟩ καὶ διὰ πειθοῦς ἐμμελοῦς [καὶ]
35 προσαγόμενον τὴν διάνοιαν τῶν ἀκουόντων καταβλητέον εἰς αὐτοὺς ὡς οἷόν τ' ἐστὶ μάλιστα· γεγυμνασμένων δ' αὐτῶν ἱκανῶς ἐν τούτοις ἐπὶ τῷ τέλει τῆς εἰς ἀρετὴν ἀγωγῆς οἱ ὅροι τῶν ἀρετῶν ἀφοριζέσθωσαν καὶ τῆς αἰτίας ἡ ἀκροτάτη παραδιδόσθω θεωρία, τελειότης τε τῶν λογισμῶν καὶ ἀναμάρτητος καί ἀνέλεγκτος ἐπιστήμη ⟨καὶ⟩ βεβαιότης ἐντιθέσθω τῆς γνώσεως, ἀλήθεια·
40 ἡ γὰρ εἰς τοῦτο ἀγωγή [τῆς παιδείας] τέλος ἔχει τῆς τῶν παίδων ἀγωγῆς τὸ κράτιστον.

---

4 τε add. Wachsmuth ‖ **9** παραδείγματα Dillon: παράδειγμα mss. ‖ **12** τε del. Usener ‖ **14** καὶ αἰσχρά add. Meineke ‖ **17** ἡγεῖσθαι L: προηγεῖσθαι Usener, ut hiatus vitaretur ‖ τοῦ del. Usener ‖ **21** νομοθετητικά L: corr. Usener ‖ **23** ἀόριστόν L: corr. Meineke | μέτρον del. Usener ‖ **24** συναρμόζει L: ἐναρμόζει Meineke ‖ **25** πότε L: τό γε Wachsmuth ‖ **26** τά add. Usener ‖ **34** lacunam signavit Usener | καί del. Usener ‖ **39** καὶ add. Wachsmuth ‖ **40** τῆς παιδείας secll. Meineke, Wachsmuth

convey in a fitting manner one's own exhortations and advice, such as bears upon each virtue, now in the form of generally accepted opinions, now in the practice of tasks, now through the performance of speeches, now in the form of admonitions as to what should or should not be done, now in the constitution of everyday life.

And when they are sufficiently schooled in these areas, one should next educate them through logical arguments, beginning from the simpler and better known and then going on, day by day and in small stages, to the explanation of the true Cause of all things. And in this connection, one must be particularly careful about not laying what requires scientific clarity of discernment before intellects that are imperfectly developed, but rather one should present to them so far as possible such arguments as are, so to speak <....> and lead on the mind of the hearers by means of well-adapted persuasion. And when they have been exercised adequately in these, at the culmination of their education in virtue, let the definitions of the virtues be laid down for them, and let the ultimate theory of the Cause of all things be conveyed to them, and let there be instilled into them perfection of reasonings, unerring and irrefutable knowledge, and firmness of understanding—in a word, truth; for it is the ascent to this that is the supreme end and purpose of the bringing up of children.

Letter 15
Πρὸς Σώπατρον περὶ ἀχαριστίας

Stobaeus, *Anth.* 2.46.16
2:262,14–23 Wachsmuth

Φευκτὴ μὲν οὖν ἐστιν ἡ ἀχαριστία δι' ἑαυτήν· ἀχθεσθείη δ' ἄν τις πρὸς αὐτὴν δικαιότερον, ἐπειδὴ κωλύει τἀγαθὸν προϊέναι καὶ ἐκφαίνεσθαι, τήν τε χώραν αὐτῷ παντελῶς ἀνατρέπει καὶ κατακλείει πως εἰς στενὸν τὰς ἔξω διαφαινομένας τῶν καλῶν ἐνεργείας, ἀποστερεῖ δὲ καὶ τὸ κοινὸν τῆς [θείας]
5 βοηθείας πάσης· διὰ τοῦτ' ἔστι πάνδεινον. παντὶ ⟨δ'⟩ ἀνδρὶ παρακελεύομαι πρῶτον, λόγον ὀρθὸν κατέχειν εὐεργεσιῶν μετὰ φιλίας· δεύτερον, εὐχαρίστως τὰς εὐεργεσίας παραλαμβάνειν καὶ προκαλεῖσθαι τὰς μείζονας εὐποιΐας διὰ τῆς εὐχαριστίας.

---

3 αὐτῷ pro αὐτῶν Dillon (deliberavit de ea re iam Wachsmuth) || 4 ἐνεργείας L: εὐεργεσίας vulg. | θείας secl. Meineke, fortasse recte || 5 δ' add. Meineke || 6 ἕνα L: πρῶτον Usener

Letter 15
To Sopater, On Ingratitude

Ingratitude is something to be avoided of its very nature, but one would have all the more reason to be indignant at it, since it prevents the good from issuing out and manifesting itself, and completely subverts its area of operation, and seriously restricts performances of noble acts from manifesting themselves externally, and deprives the world in general of all [divine] assistance. For this reason it is a very great evil. I would first of all exhort every man to keep an accurate record of benefits received in connection with friendship, and, second, to accept benefactions with gratitude and to call forth even greater acts of beneficence through such gratitude.

Letter 16
Πρὸς Σώπατρον περὶ ἀρετῆς

Fragment 1
Stobaeus, *Anth.* 3.1.17
3:9,5-10 Hense

Ψυχῆς μὲν οὖν ἂν εἴη ἀρετὴ τελειότης καὶ εὐμετρία τῆς ζωῆς, λόγου τε καὶ νοῦ καὶ διανοήσεως ἡ ἀκροτάτη καὶ καθαρωτάτη ἐνέργεια. τὰ δ' ἔργα τῆς ἀρετῆς ἀγαθοειδῆ, κάλλιστα, νοερά, σπουδαῖα, πλήρη μεσότητος, εὐκαιρίας μετέχοντα, προηγούμενα, τέλους ἀρίστου στοχαζόμενα, χαρίεντα
5 ὅτι μάλιστα θεωρείσθω.

Fragment 2
Stobaeus, *Anth.* 3.1.49
3:19,6-20,9 Hense

Οὐκοῦν καὶ διὰ νοῦ καθαροῦ καὶ ἀπολυομένου πάσης σωματοειδοῦς διαμορφώσεως ἡ θέα τῆς ἀρετῆς περιγίγνεται· τὸ δ' ὁποῖον τί ἐστιν ὧδε ἄν τις καταμάθοι· κάλλος καὶ συμμετρία καὶ ἀλήθεια, ταυτότης τε ἀμετάστατος καὶ ἁπλότης, ἐξῃρημένη τε ἀπὸ τῶν ἄλλων ὑπεροχή, τελειότης τε
5 ἀνυπέρβλητος καὶ ἀκρότης τῶν ὄντων, καθαρότης τε ὑπεραίρουσα πάντα καὶ ἄμικτος. ἰδὲ ἅπαντα τὰ τοιαῦτα ἔνδειγμα αὐτοῦ παρέχεται ἱκανόν. ὁπότε δὴ οὖν τὸ νοητὸν εἶδος κατίδοις τῆς ἀρετῆς, θεώρει τοῦτο λοιπὸν ἀφ' ἑαυτοῦ περὶ πᾶσαν ζωὴν ἀμερίστως μεριζόμενον τρόπον τινὰ τοιοῦτον, ὡς πληθυομένων τῶν μεταλαμβανόντων μένειν αὐτὸ ἕν, καὶ πάντῃ μεριζομένων ⟨τῶν⟩ περὶ
10 αὐτὸ ἀμέριστον αὐτὸ ὑπάρχειν, καὶ γιγνομένων καὶ ἀπολλυμένων ἐκείνων ἀγέννητον αὐτὸ εἶναι καὶ ἄφθαρτον, καὶ εἰς ἀνομοιότητα προχωρούντων τὸ αὐτὸ ἀεὶ διαμένειν μήτε κινούμενον ἀπὸ τῆς προόδου τῶν γιγνομένων μήτε διιστάμενον ἀφ' ἑαυτοῦ διὰ τὴν ἐν πᾶσι τοῖς διεστηκόσι παρουσίαν μήτε αὐτοῖς συμφερόμενον ἢ συναυξανόμενον ἤ τινα ἄλλην ἀπ' αὐτῶν δεχόμενον
15 ἀλλοίωσιν. καίτοι οὕτως αὐτὸ κατόψει τὸ αὐτὸ ὅλον ἐν πᾶσι παρὸν μετὰ τοῦ μένειν ἑκάστου τὴν οὐσίαν τῶν μετεχόντων καὶ κατὰ τὴν οἰκείαν ὑπόστασιν ἕκαστον βέλτιστον γίγνεσθαι. κατὰ δὴ τοῦτον τὸν λόγον καὶ τοὺς ἀνθρώπους

Letter 16
To Sopater, On Virtue

Fragment 1

Virtue might be described as the perfection of the soul and proper balance of its life and as the highest and purest activity of reason and intellect and discursive intelligence. Let the acts of virtue be taken, above all, as being boniform, excellently fine, intellectual, noble, full of moderation, participant in appropriateness, promoting moral advancement, aiming at the best end, and graceful.

Fragment 2

So it is through an intellect that is pure and free from all bodily influences to mold it that the vision of virtue comes about. The quality of this one may grasp as being the following: beauty, symmetry and truth, unchanging identity and simplicity, a transcendent superiority to all other things, unsurpassable perfection and the summit of existence, and a purity that is raised above all other things and unmixed with them. And as to the fact that all its qualities are such as I have described, one sufficient indication may be provided. Whenever you contemplate the intelligible form of virtue, think of this as divided indivisibly from itself about the whole realm of living things in some such manner as the following, that, while the things that participate in it are multifarious, it itself remains one; and whereas all the things about it are divided in every way, it itself is undivided; and while they come into being and perish, it itself is ungenerated and imperishable; and while they proceed into unlikeness, it continues always the same, neither moved as a result of the procession from it of all that comes to be, nor separated from itself by reason of its presence in all those things that have separated themselves from it, nor being borne about with them, nor sharing in their increase, nor receiving from them any other type of alteration.

Thus, then, you will see it as present as a whole the same in all things, along with assuring the permanence of the essence of each of the things participating in it, and each of them attaining the best state consistent with its proper character. And in accordance with this principle it adorns men with the finest gifts, with the highest intellectual activities,

διακοσμεῖ τοῖς καλλίστοις δώροις, νοεραῖς μὲν ἐνεργείαις ἀκροτάταις, λόγοις δὲ τῆς ψυχῆς τελειοτάτοις, ζωῆς δὲ δυνάμεσιν ὑπερεχούσαις πᾶσαν γένεσιν.

6 ἄμικτος· ἰδὲ ἅπαντα τὰ τοιαῦτα ἔνδειγμα αὐτοῦ παρέχεται ἱκανόν· ὁπότε Rhode liter. Centralbl. A. 1883 p. 487, ἄμικτος· εἰ δὲ ἅπαντα τὰ τοιαῦτα, ἓν δεῖγμα αὐτοῦ παρέχεται ἱκανόν· ὁπότε mss. || 9 πάντῃ scripsit Hense: παντὶ Br | Hense ad loc.: "τῶν addidit Rhode, sed praestat fortasse πάντων μ. π. αὐτὸ"|| 14 συμφερόμενον: συναφαιρούμενον ci. Hense, συμφθινόμενον ci. Rhode | ἀπ' αὐτῶν Thomas: ἁπάντων Br 18 ὅροις: δώροις mavult Thomas

Fragment 3
Stobaeus, *Anth.* 3.37.32
3:706,3–6 Hense

Ἀγαθὸς νομιζέσθω ὁ τὴν τελειοτάτην κατὰ τὸν χωριστὸν νοῦν ἐνέργειαν διασῴζων καὶ τὴν μετουσίαν τοῦ νοητοῦ κάλλους παραδεχόμενος καὶ τῆς τοῦ θεοῦ οὐσίας καὶ δυνάμεως μέτοχος.

Fragment 4
Stobaeus, *Anth.* 4.39.23
5:907,7–9 Hense

Εὐδαίμων ἐστὶν ὁ θεῷ κατὰ τὸ δυνατὸν ὅμοιος, τέλειος, ἁπλοῦς, καθαρός, ἐξῃρημένος ἀπὸ τῆς ἀνθρωπίνης ζωῆς.

2 ἐξῃρημένος Wyttenbach et Wakefield: ἐξηρτημένος M A Tr. ἐξηρτημένης per compend. S. cf. Stob. Anth. vol. V (ed. Hense) p. 910, 17 adn.

with the most perfect psychic reason-principles, and with powers of life that transcend the whole realm of generation.

Fragment 3

Let that man be accounted good who pursues the most perfect activity in accordance with transcendent intellect, opening himself up to the presence of intelligible beauty and being participant in the essence and power of God.

Fragment 4

He is happy who is as like as possible to God, perfect, simple, pure, and transcendent over human life.

Letter 17
Πρὸς Σώπατρον περὶ αἰδοῦς

Stobaeus, *Anth.* 3.31.9
3:671,2–5 Hense

Τοιαῦτα δ᾽ ἂν εἴη καὶ τὰ τῆς αἰδοῦς ἀντεχόμενα, τιμῶντα δὲ τὰ χρηστὰ ἤθη, δι᾽ ἣν τῶν αἰσχρῶν πάντων ἀπεχόμεθα· τὴν δ᾽ ἀναίδειαν ἐξορίζοντα τῆς ψυχῆς, δι᾽ ἣν ὑπὸ τῶν αἰσχρῶν οἱ πολλοὶ ἁλίσκονται.

Letter 18
Πρὸς Σώπατρον περὶ ἀληθείας

Stobaeus, *Anth.* 3.11.35
3:443,6–17 Hense

Ἀλήθεια μέν, ὥσπερ καὶ τοὔνομα δηλοῖ, περὶ θεοὺς ποιεῖ τὴν ἐπιστροφὴν καὶ τῶν θεῶν τὴν ἀκήρατον ἐνέργειαν· ἡ δὲ δοξομιμητικὴ αὕτη εἰδωλοποιία, ὥς φησι Πλάτων, περὶ τὸ ἄθεον καὶ σκοτεινὸν πλανᾶται. καὶ ἡ μὲν τοῖς νοητικοῖς εἴδεσι καὶ θείοις καὶ τοῖς ὄντως οὖσι καὶ κατὰ τὰ αὐτὰ ἀεὶ ἔχουσι
5 τελεοῦται, ἡ δὲ τὸ ἀνείδεον καὶ μὴ ὂν καὶ ἄλλοτε ἄλλως ἔχον ἀποβλέπει καὶ περὶ αὐτοῦ ἀμβλυώττει. καὶ ἡ μὲν αὐτὸ ὅ ἐστι θεωρεῖ, ἡ δ᾽ οἷον φαίνεται τοῖς πολλοῖς τοιοῦτον ὑποδύεται πρόσχημα. διόπερ δὴ ἡ μὲν πρὸς νοῦν ὁμιλεῖ καὶ τὸ ἐν ἡμῖν νοερὸν αὔξει, ἡ δὲ τῷ ἀεὶ δοκοῦντι θηρεύεται τὴν ἄνοιαν καὶ ἐξαπατᾷ.

Letter 17
To Sopater, On Self-Respect

Such, then, would be the type of conduct that maintains self-respect, honoring good habits of life, by virtue of which we abstain from all foul practices, and excluding from the soul shamelessness, through which the majority of men are ensnared by foul practices.

Letter 18
To Sopater, On Truth

Truth, as indeed the name indicates, turns itself toward the gods and the unsullied activity of the gods, but this image-making art that is productive of appearances, to use Plato's term (*Soph.* 267e), wanders around in godless darkness. And the former finds its completion in the sphere of the intellective and divine forms and the realm of those beings that are truly real and always in the same state, while the latter looks to what is formless and nonexistent and always in a different state, and blinds itself with that. The former contemplates what is truly existent, whereas the latter assumes such an appearance as corresponds to the imagination of the many. For this reason, then, the former consorts with intellect and increases the intellectual element in us, whereas the latter, by the constant employment of appearances, seeks out mindlessness and practices deception upon it.

Letter 19
Πρὸς ἄγνωστόν τινα περὶ γάμου χρήσεως

Stobaeus, Anth. 4.33.57
4:587,14–588,2 Hense

Οὐκοῦν καὶ περὶ τοῦ ἄρχειν μὲν τὸν ἄρρενα ἄρχεσθαι δὲ τὴν θήλειαν ὁμογνωμονήσουσιν. τὸ δὲ σχῆμα τῆς ἀρχῆς ἔσται οὐχ οἷον τὸ δεσποτικόν, θεραπεῦον τὸ τοῦ κρείττονος συμφέρον· οὐδ' οἷον τὸ τῶν τεχνῶν, μόνου τοῦ ἥττονος ἐπιμελούμενον· ἀλλ' οἷον τὸ πολιτικόν, κηδόμενον ἐξ ἴσου τοῦ κοινῇ
5   συμφέροντος.

4 κοινῇ A: κοινοῦ S M

Letter 20
Πρὸς ἄγνωστόν τινα περὶ ἀρχῆς (?)

Stobaeus, Anth. 4.5.62
4:219,4–9 Hense

Πᾶν γὰρ τὸ τιμώμενον αὔξεται, ἐλαττοῦται δὲ τὸ ἀτιμαζόμενον· καὶ τοῦτό ἐστι τὸ διαφανέστατον σημεῖον ἀρχῆς εὖ διοικουμένης. προτρέπει τε γὰρ τοὺς ἀρχομένους ἐπὶ τὰ καλὰ ἐπιτηδεύματα, ⟨ὡς⟩ καὶ τὴν ἐπιβάλλουσαν ἀξίαν ἑκάστοις διανέμει, καὶ πληροῖ τὰς πόλεις τῶν ἀρίστων
5   ἐπιτηδευμάτων.

3 ὡς add. Hense

Letter 19
To an Unknown Recipient, On Marriage

So on the question of the male ruling and the female being ruled they will be of one mind. The form of this rule, however, will not be like that of master over slave, serving the interest of the stronger; nor like that proper to the arts, which has care only for the inferior element; but rather analogous to political rule, which pays equal heed to the common interest of both.

Letter 20
To an Unknown Recipient, On Ruling (?)

For everything that is honored flourishes, whereas what is given no honor tends to diminish, and this is the most conspicuous sign of a well-administered regime. For it exhorts its subjects toward noble practices, even as it apportions to each his proper worth, and it fills cities with the best sort of practices.

Testimonium 1
Πρὸς ἄγνωστόν τινα περὶ καθόδου ψυχῶν (?)

T 1
Damascius, *In Phaed.* 203,26–204,3 Norvin

Πῶς ὁ Ἰάμβλιχος τὸ ἐνάντιον φησὶ παρὰ τῶν τελέως ἀποκαθισταμένων; ἢ τὰ ἀντίστροφα πάντα ἐροῦμεν, οὐδέποτε κατιέναι αὐτάς, ἢ κατά τινα περίοδον καθόδων αἰτίαν οὐκ ἔχουσιν ἀναγκαίαν, ἢ ὅσον γε ἐπὶ τῇ οἰκείᾳ ζωῇ μὴ ῥεπούσῃ πρὸς γένεσιν, ἢ τὸ τρίτον κατὰ τὸ εἶδος τῆς ζωῆς ἀγένητον
5 ποιουμένης τὴν κάθοδον καὶ πρὸς τὰ ἐκεῖ ἀδιάκοπον, ὡς καὶ αὐτὸς ἐν ἐπιστολαῖς γράφει, ὑπὲρ τοῦ οἰκείου λόγου ἀπολογούμενος τὸν τρίτον ῥηθέντα τρόπον.

Testimonium 2

T 2
Olympiodorus, *In Gorg.* 46.9.20–28 Westerink

Ἐπεὶ τοίνυν καὶ ταῦτα καλῶς εἴρηται, ἄξιον ζητῆσαι τί δήποτε, ὡς λέλεκται, τριῶν οὐσῶν νεκυιῶν, φαίνεται ὁ Ἰάμβλιχος ἔν τινι αὐτοῦ ἐπιστολῇ τῶν δύο μόνων μνημονεύων, τῆς τε τῷ Φαίδωνι καὶ τῆς ἐν τῇ Πολιτείᾳ, ταύτης δὲ οὔ. Φάμεν οὖν ὅτι ἴσως ὁ ἄνθρωπος πρὸς ὃν ἐποιεῖτο
5 τὴν ἐπιστολήν, περὶ τούτων τῶν δύο νεκυιῶν ἦν αὐτὸν αἰτήσας εἰπεῖν τι, καὶ διὰ τοῦτο ἐκείνων μόνον ἐμνήσθη· οὐ γὰρ ὁ τηλικοῦτος φιλόσοφος ἠγνόει ταύτην.

Testimonium 1
To an Unknown Recipient, On the Descent of Souls (?)

How does Iamblichus say the opposite of souls who have been restored to a state of perfection? Shall we say just the converse about them, that they never descend either in accordance with a certain cycle of descents that involves no necessitating cause, or inasmuch as the mode of life proper to them does not incline toward the realm of generation, or, third, by reason of the form of their life which makes for a descent that does not involve generation and that never breaks its connection with the higher realm, as he himself writes also in his *Letters*, explaining his own theory along the third line of argument above-mentioned.

Testimonium 2

Since, then, this has been well said, it is worth raising the question as to why, when, as we have said, there are actually three myths of the afterlife, Iamblichus is observed, in a letter of his, to make mention of only two, that in the *Phaedo* and that in the *Republic*, but not of this one (sc. in the *Gorgias*). Our reply is that perhaps the man to whom he addressed the letter was only asking him to say something about the former two myths and that that is the reason why he only discussed them; for a philosopher of his caliber would not have been ignorant of this one.

Commentary

Letter 1: To Agrippa, On Ruling

The identity of Agrippa cannot be established with certainty, but he is not listed among Iamblichus's disciples, and, especially in view of the subject matter, it is likely that, like Dyscolius below, he is a member of the imperial administration or of the local aristocracy, probably in Syria, but possibly further afield in Asia Minor. The fact that Agrippa was a name taken by dynasts of Judea in the first century C.E. might indicate that it continued to be held by prominent figures in Syrian society in Iamblichus's day.

The themes raised in the letter are pretty basic, it must be said, but are yet worthy of comment in some respects. The suggestion that the inevitably dominant nature of ruling should be tempered by φιλανθρωπία is to be found in the treatise of "Archytas" *On Law and Justice*, a fragment of which is preserved by Stobaeus just a few pages earlier in the same chapter of the *Anthologia* (4.5.61 = frg. 5 Thesleff). There Archytas declares that "the true ruler should not only be knowledgeable and competent in the art of good rule but also imbued with sympathy for his fellow-men [φιλάνθρωπος]." Archytas continues by saying that "the ruler should also be law-abiding [νόμιμος]," which is very much the theme of fragment 2 of this letter.

In Plato, *Symp.* 196c, it is said that love needs to be ruled by temperance (σωφροσύνη), but also that love exercises a pleasant rule over willing subjects. Ἔρως is absent here, but maybe φιλανθρωπία serves as its replacement; see also φιλεῖται in fragment 1.5. Plato, *Leg.* 3.690b–c, specifies that rule needs to be exercised without force over willing subjects in order that this rule may be acceptable. *Leg.* 10.890a also, as well as *Prot.* 337d and *Gorg.* 484b, have the dichotomy between νόμος and φύσις as their topic. This passage is important in our context, since according to *Leg.* 10.890a there are things that are beautiful (καλά) by nature (φύσει) or by convention (νόμῳ). If Iamblichus has this passage in mind, this allusion would perhaps explain why he introduces beauty in this context.

The wording of fragment 1 suggests that Iamblichus's argument is close to the notion that one should keep the middle ground between extremes.

Fragment 1.1. ὑπεροχή. See Aristotle, *Pol.* 1295b14: Excess of every kind is bad. Excess of wealth, for example, leads to an unwillingness to be governed. Iamblichus approaches the issue from the other side, so to speak. In the passage that surrounds 1295b14, Aristotle advocates that the middle class should rule in order to avoid both tyranny and extreme democracy.

Fragment 1.2. τὸ ὑπέρογκον. See Plato, *Leg.* 5.728e. According to Plato, too, excessive wealth and property create enmities and discord. Plato calls for a mitigation of excess. Iamblichus uses ὑπέρογκον, we may note, adverbially, at *Protr.* 14; 77,18 Pistelli: ὑπέρογκον φρονοῦντες.

Fragment 1.3. τὸ αὐστηρόν. In Aristotle's view, this is something that needs to be balanced. See *Eth. eud.* 1240a2.

Fragment 1.4. εὐπρόσιτον. Εὐπρόσιτος in the sense of "easy of access," "approachable," seems not to be attested before the second century C.E., for example, Galen, *Prop. an.* 8; Alexander Aphrodisiensis, *In Top.* 531.21.

Fragment 2.1. πάντων βασιλεὺς ὁ νόμος. This sentiment goes back all the way to Pindar (frg. 169a), but it was widely quoted, notably by Herodotus (3.38.4) and Plato in *Gorg.* 484b, *Leg.* 3.690b-c and 10.890a, *Symp.* 196c, *Prot.* 337d, and *Ep.* 8.354b-c. See also Aristides 2.68 and Iamblichus, *Protr.* 20 (100,16-17 Pistelli).

Fragment 2.6. τὰς διοικήσεις τῶν πόλεων. See *Symp.* 196c, where the sophist Alcidamas is credited with being the author of the phrase οἱ πόλεως βασιλεῖς νόμοι. See Aristotle, *Rhet.* 1406a18-23, where he also attributes the phrase to Alcidamas: οἱ τῶν πόλεων βασιλεῖς νόμοι.

Fragment 2.8. κοινὸν ἀγαθὸν ὁ νόμος. That the law should be something universal for every citizen is, naturally, a very common thought in Plato. See, e.g., *Leg.* 1.644d-645a, where law is presented as the "golden cord" that leads the citizens to virtue.

Fragment 2.13. ἀδιάφθορον εἶναι ... εἰς δύναμιν ἀνθρωπίνην. This phrase is almost identical with Plato, *Leg.* 6.768b, where it is said of judges that they should be as incorruptible as humanly possible.

Letter 2: To Anatolius, On Justice

The only Anatolius whom we know of in relation to Iamblichus is the man who is reported by Eunapius (*Vit. phil.* 457–458) to have been his teacher before Porphyry and who in some sense "ranked next after" (τὰ δεύτερα φερομένῳ) Porphyry (perhaps being second in command at his school). It may seem slightly odd, perhaps, to dedicate a letter of this sort to one's old teacher, but there it is. Porphyry also dedicates a work, the *Homeric Investigations* ('Ομηρικὰ ζητήματα), to Anatolius, but that is more natural.

The description of justice here as τέλος and συναγωγή of all the virtues is notable, but we can find no suitable analogies in the literature. It could, however, be taken as a summary description of the role of justice in Plato's *Republic*.

Fragment 1.2. κατὰ τὸν παλαιὸν λόγον. The reference is to Phocylides, frg. 17 Bergk: ἐν δὲ δικαιοσύνῃ συλλήβδην πᾶσ' ἀρετὴ ἔνι, quoted by Aristotle, *Eth. nic.* 1129b27, which is probably from where Iamblichus gets it. The scholiast ad loc., who actually attributes it to Theognis, remarks that it has taken on the role of a proverb and adduces also Theophrastus, in the first book of his work *On Characters* (not the surviving work) and in the first book of his *Ethics*.

Fragment 2.4–5. εὐσύμβολα καὶ εὐσυνάλλακτα. This is a typical stylistic collocution, of which one finds so many in the works of Philo Judaeus or Plutarch, for example, a pair of virtual synonyms, the latter being somewhat rarer than the former. This pair, however, seems to occur nowhere else in extant literature. The former adjective is attested in this sense already in Xenophon (*Mem.* 2.6.5), whereas the latter does not occur before Plutarch (*Mor.* 42F).

Fragment 2.5: κωλυτικά. Porphyry, *Abst.* 2.47. See also Aristotle, *Eth. nic.* 1096b12: good things prevent their opposites (cf. line 6 of this fragment). The opposite is also true, as in Xenophon, *Mem.* 4.5.7: ἀκρασία prevents us from doing what we need to do.

Letter 3: To Arete, On Self-Control

The lady Arete may well be identical with the Arete, now an old lady, whose troubles with her neighbors in Phrygia are referred to by the emperor Julian in his *Letter to Themistius*, 259D. We may suppose that she is a member of the local aristocracy and reasonably well read in the classics of literature and philosophy, so as to be able to appreciate the references made here by Iamblichus. Note that her name is not the same as that of the queen of the Phaeacians in the *Odyssey*, since that lady was Ἀρήτη and Iamblichus's addressee is Ἀρετή, "Virtue," making her that much more suitable as a recipient of this letter.

The first fragment of the letter seems to begin, not quite at the beginning, but near it. Having made some mention of σωφροσύνη itself, to the effect, perhaps, that it operates properly in the area of ἐπιθυμία, Iamblichus moves to generalize its range of influence, by defining it as εὐκοσμία, or "orderliness" in the relations of the three parts of the Platonist soul, reason, spiritedness (θυμός), and the passions, to one another—these denominated, we may note, not as μέρη, "parts," as in Plato's original exposition of them in *Resp.* 4, but, with greater "correctness," δυνάμεις, "powers"—a result of many centuries of discussion in philosophical circles as to whether the soul has "parts," beginning, perhaps, with Posidonius and culminating in the treatise by Iamblichus's own teacher, Porphyry, *On the Powers of the Soul* (frg. 251–55 Smith). The modification from μέρη to δυνάμεις is discussed in particular in fragment 253.

The following fragments seem to present a relatively austere view of the nature of virtue, as tending to ἀπάθεια, the suppression of the passions, rather than μετριοπάθεια, their moderation. In fragment 2, at any rate, we seem to be confronted with the "purificatory" virtues, in terms of the scheme laid down by Plotinus in *Enn.* 1.2 (and elaborated further by Porphyry in *Sent.* 32), which call for ἀπάθεια, as opposed to the "civic" virtues, which entertain μετριοπάθεια. The implication of rejecting the "mortal element" (which refers here, not primarily to the body, but to the lower parts of the soul, termed "mortal" in the *Timaeus* [41d]) is that the true purpose of the practice of the virtues is divinization (see Plotinus, *Enn.* 1.2.6). We may note the significant quotations from Plato, in particular that from the *Phaedo*, which reinforce this position, as do the striking images of Bellerophon and the Chimaera in fragment 3, and Perseus and the Gorgon in fragment 4. We have found no other examples of the allegorization of these myths in this sense.

In fragment 6, σωφροσύνη is presented—as indeed justice is in *Letter 2*—as that which harmonizes all the other virtues and which indeed preserves them in being. This power of σωφροσύνη is then, in a somewhat hyperbolic vein, extended in fragment 7 to the whole cosmos, as the harmonizer of the seasons and the elements.

Fragment 1.2. τὴν συμμετρίαν αὐτῶν πρὸς ἀλλήλας. See Plato, *Soph.* 228c: ὑπὸ συμμετρίας τῆς πρὸς ἄλληλα.

Fragment 1.2–3. εὐταξίαν θυμοῦ τε καὶ ἐπιθυμίας καὶ λόγου. The term εὐταξία is used in the context of the struggle between the three parts of the soul in *Soph.* 228b. See also Plato, *Def.* 411d: εὐταξία τῶν τῆς ψυχῆς μερῶν πρὸς ἄλληλα.

Fragment 1.3. τάξιν. On the terminology, see Gorgias, *Hel.* 14: τάξις τῆς ψυχῆς.

Fragment 1.3: εὐκοσμίαν. There may be some reminiscence here of Plato, *Prot.* 325d–e, where Protagoras specifies that εὐκοσμία is what children are sent to school to learn, above all other, more particular, subjects.

Fragment 1.5: πολυειδής. Σωφροσύνη is presumably given this epithet because it has to preside over the multifariousness of the passions (cf. τὸ δεινὸν ... καὶ πολυειδὲς θρέμμα referring to the passionate part of the soul at *Resp.* 9.590a). Also, at *Phd.* 80b, the divine is characterized as μονοειδής, the human as πολυειδής. See also *Phdr.* 238a, where ὕβρις is described as πολυμελὲς καὶ πολυμερές.

Fragment 2.1. τὸ θνητοειδές. The mortal is a burden to the immortal. At *Phd.* 86a, this fact is illustrated by the example of the lyre and its "perishable" chords and the eternal harmony (cf. frg. 6.3).

Fragment 2.3: τὰς προσηλούσας τῷ σώματι … ἡδονάς. This is a reference to *Phd.* 83d: ὅτι ἑκάστη ἡδονὴ καὶ λύπη ὥσπερ ἧλον ἔχουσα προσηλοῖ αὐτὴν πρὸς τὸ σῶμα. Iamblichus also makes reference to this at *Vit. Pyth.* 32.228, where he speaks of passions "nailing" the soul to the body.

Fragment 2.3-4: ἐν ἁγνοῖς βάθροις βεβῶσα. This quotation of *Phdr.* 254b is interesting in that it refers in the dialogue to the vision of Absolute Beauty, to which σωφροσύνη is here being assimilated (although σωφροσύνη is there associated with Beauty). See Plotinus, *Enn.* 1.6.9.15: ἕως ἂν ἴδῃς σωφροσύνην ἐν ἁγνῷ βεβῶσαν βάθρῳ, where the reference to beauty is suppressed.

Fragment 3.1. τελέους. See *Leg.* 929c: This adjective (τελείος) also can be used to describe the adult human being.

Fragment 3.1. τὸ ἀτελές. The adjective has the meaning of "indeterminate" in Plato, *Phileb.* 24b; it is also, however, used of minors: see Aristotle, *Pol.* 1275a17. Both senses are relevant here. Taken together with the previous note, it becomes apparent that Iamblichus sees self-control in connection with the development of the human being to well-rounded adulthood.

Fragment 3.1. τὸ ἐμπαθές. See Plotinus, *Enn.* 4.7.13 and 5.9.4, where it is τὸ ἐμπαθές that differentiates soul from intellect and leads it downward to organize Matter.

Fragment 3.2-3: τὸν Βελλεροφόντην ἐννοήσας. This adducing of Bellerophon's slaying of the Chimaera is most interesting. The Chimaera is presented as a symbol of the passionate part of the soul, characterized memorably by Plato in *Resp.* 9.588c as a many-headed beast, "like the Chimaera, Scylla, Cerberus and so on, whose form is a composite of the features of more than one creature." Whether or not Iamblichus himself is the first to pick up this allusion and run with it we cannot be certain, but the bringing in of Bellerophon as σωφροσύνη, "slayer" of the passions, is an original development.

Fragment 3.3. τῆς κοσμιότητος. The terms κοσμιότης and σωφροσύνη are connected in *Gorg.* 508a, where the doctrine is attributed by Socrates to "the wise" that the cosmos is held together by these two qualities, together with some others, namely, κοινωνία, φιλία, and δικαιότης.

Fragment 3.3. συναγωνιζόμενος. It seems better to read the nominative masculine, as suggested by Meineke, referring to Bellerophon, rather than the genitive feminine of the manuscript, referring to "good order" (κοσμιότης). The manuscript reading is possible but awkward and can easily be taken as a scribal error.

Fragment 4.2. κατὰ τὴν Κράτητος γνώμην. This saying of (presumably) the Cynic philosopher Crates of Thebes is not otherwise recorded (= frg. 45 Mullach). Hense suggests that this may originally have been a line of iambic verse—Σώζει μὲν οἴκους ἥδε, σώζει καὶ πόλεις—which is not a bad suggestion, since Crates is known to have composed verses and even tragedies. At any rate, Iamblichus will almost certainly have picked this up as a tag from some previous philosophical source rather than from the man himself.

Fragment 4.3–4: Περσεὺς ... τὴν Γοργόνα. This allegorization of the myth does not appear to be attested elsewhere, though Gorgons in the plural are presented as examples of myths that need correction in *Phdr.* 229d— as indeed are Pegasuses.

Fragment 4.5. καθέλκουσαν. This verb apparently serves in Plato only to describe the dragging of ships into the sea: *Leg.* 4.706d and *Hipp. min.* 370d. However, Plotinus uses the verb at *Enn.* 2.9.2.8 to describe the lower parts of the soul being "dragged down" to Matter and likewise at *Enn.* 4.3.6.26.

Fragment 4.5. ἀπολιθοῦσαν. The only occurrence of this verb in Plato apparently is attested in the codex Vindobonensis 55, suppl. phil. gr. 39 [F] at *Tim.* 60d (ἀπολιθουμένω). Since its meaning does not easily fit the context, editors of the *Timaeus* normally do not follow the reading of this codex but read ἀπομονουμένω. Otherwise, the first usage attested occurs in the Aristotelian *Prob.* 937a17.

Fragment 4.6. πλησμονῇ. As *Resp.* 9.571e and 586d show, in Plato's view πλησμονή always needs to be avoided—just like its opposite—in regard to everything (e.g., food, just as with ἐπιθυμίαι) in order to achieve a life that, among other things, is directed toward keeping τὸ θυμοειδές and τὸ ἐπιθυμητικόν under control.

Fragment 5.1-2: κρηπὶς τῆς ἀρετῆς, ὡς ἔλεγε Σωκράτης, ἡ ἐγκράτειά ἐστι τῆς γλυκυθυμίας. This is a phrase taken from Xenophon's *Mem.* 1.5.4, part of a discourse on self-control, for which Xenophon's term is ἐγκράτεια rather than σωφροσύνη. The rather rare word γλυκυθυμία, here translated "self-indulgence," however, does not occur in the Xenophontic passage but may be borrowed from Plato, *Leg.* 635c. It also occurs at *Myst.* 5.11.214, used to describe the "attractiveness" of matter.

Fragment 5.2: κόσμος δὲ τῶν ἀγαθῶν πάντων. This seems to be a reference to *Resp.* 4.430e, where, however, Plato is making the point that σωφροσύνη imposes order on all the pleasures and desires rather than that it is an adornment of all goods.

Fragment 5.3: ἀσφάλεια δὲ τῶν καλλίστων ἕξεων. This is a rather quaint touch by Iamblichus, setting his own definition beside those of Socrates and Plato; ἀσφάλεια in the sense, presumably, of "preservation" or "secure maintenance."

Fragment 6.4. ἀφορμὴν παρέχει. For the phrase, see Demosthenes 18.156; see also Philemon frg. 110 Kock: πάντων ἀφορμή τῶν καλῶν—where, admittedly, the context is rather pseudo-philosophical.

Fragment 7.1. ἡ τῶν ὡρῶν τοῦ ἐναντίου σύστασις. For just the same phrase, see *Symp.* 188a. The context of that passage and its content, however, while closely related, is different in detail.

Fragment 7.1-2. ἡ τῶν στοιχείων πρὸς ἄλληλα σύγκρασις. See Asclepius apud *Placita philosophorum* 5.21.2: σύγκρασις τῶν στοιχείων (sc. of heat and cold).

Fragment 7.3. διὰ τὴν κοσμιότητα τῶν καλλίστων μέτρων κόσμος ἐπικαλεῖται. For this "definition" of σωφροσύνη, see fragment 5 above.

Letter 4: To Asphalius, On Wisdom

This passage sounds as if it might come from the beginning of a letter. Of Asphalius, nothing is known. He is not named as a pupil.

The word here translated "wisdom," φρόνησις, would normally be more correctly rendered by "practical wisdom," as opposed to σοφία, but that is an Aristotelian distinction that Iamblichus does not appear to be making here. It is rather the Platonic use of the word, as the virtue proper to the rational part of the soul, the λογιστικόν, that he has in mind. The reference to it as an ὄμμα νοερόν, overseeing all the others, reinforces this impression. The whole thrust of this passage is that φρόνησις is that which assimilates us to God (πρὸς θεοὺς ἡμῖν κοινωνία, ... πρὸς αὐτοὺς ἀφομοιούμεθα, lines 7–9). The assertion of its contemplation of νοῦς is somewhat ambiguous, as between our own intellect and the hypostasis of Intellect, but such phrases as ἀπὸ τοῦ καθαροῦ καὶ τελείου νοῦ (lines 4–5) and εἰς αὐτὸν τὸν νοῦν (line 5) would seem to favor the latter alternative. Certainly it is portrayed as having a practical aspect, directing cities and men in the right direction, but that is in the direction of divinity, so it is practical in the way that the wisdom of the Guardians of the *Republic* is practical.

Line 2. ὄμμα νοερόν. This is a variant of the Platonic expression τὸ τῆς ψυχῆς ὄμμα (*Resp.* 7.533d), but although it occurs in various later writers, such as Synesius (*Ep.* 154.86), Syrianus (*In Met.* 25,6 Kroll), and Dionysius the Areopagite (*Cael. hier.* 15; 50,13 Heil-Ritter), it is not found before Iamblichus.

Lines 2–3. κατὰ τὴν ἐγκαιροτάτην διάθεσιν. First of all, it seems better to read κατὰ for the καί of the manuscripts, accepted by Hense; to have διάθεσιν as coordinate with τάξεις τε καὶ μέτρα is possible but clumsier. Ἔγκαιρος is a thoroughly Platonic word, the superlative occurring at *Leg.* 4.717a but not in conjunction with διάθεσις.

Line 10. διάγνωσις. On the use of the phrase, see Demosthenes 18.128: καλῶν ἢ μὴ τοιούτων τίς διάγνωσις. In Plato's *Leg.* 11.936a the duty of διάγνωσις falls to the educator who has to decide between the right and the wrong kind of jesting.

Lines 14–15. διαζωγραφεῖ ..., τὸ μὲν ἐξαλείφουσα, τὸ δὲ ἐναπομοργνυμένη. The verb διαζωγραφεῖ may be derived ultimately from such a passage as Plato, *Tim.* 55e, while the rest of the phrase seems to be a variant on *Resp.* 6.501b: τὸ μὲν ἂν οἶμαι ἐξαλείφοιεν, τὸ δὲ πάλιν ἐγγράφοιεν.

Line 15: ἐναπομόργνυμι is a very rare word, not occurring in extant literature before Porphyry (*Sent.* 29).

Letter 5: To Dexippus, On Dialectic

This praise of dialectic is directed, very suitably, to Iamblichus's pupil, Dexippus, of whom we still have a short commentary, in question and answer form, on Aristotle's *Categories*. It may be compared with his other letter on Dialectic, to Sopater (*Letter* 13, below). This extract sounds rather as if it comes from the beginning of the letter, to judge from the rather portentous opening, reminiscent both of the beginning of Plato's *Laws* and of the passage near the beginning of the *Philebus* (16c), where the method of διαίρεσις (which Iamblichus can take as applying equally well to dialectic as a whole) is described as "a gift of the gods to men" (θεῶν εἰς ἀνθρώπους δόσις).

If this latter passage is an influence, however, Iamblichus changes the god concerned, not unsuitably, from Prometheus to Hermes, as the patron of rational discourse (ὁ λόγιος). He continues, then, with references to Calliope, then to Apollo, both as the god of Delphi and the god of Branchidae, his riddling prophecies being viewed as incitements to dialectical reasoning. This is Iamblichus in an unusually cultured mode, and most impressive as such.

The equation here of dialectic with either philosophy as a whole or at least its most essential part may usefully be compared with the praise of dialectic contained in Plotinus's little essay, *Enn.* 1.3, *On Dialectic*, with which Iamblichus was probably acquainted.

Line 1. Θεὸς ἦν τις. As suggested above, apart from the allusion to *Phileb.* 16c, this may embody an echo of the beginning of the *Laws* (624a): Θεός, ὦ ξένε, θεός. There may also be a reminiscence intended of the passage in *Phdr.* 274d–275b, describing the invention of writing by the god Theuth.

Line 2. ὁ λόγιος Ἑρμῆς. This title for Hermes is of somewhat mysterious origin. It occurs also in Lucian, *Pseudol.* 24 and *Apol.* 2; in Philostratus, *Vit. Apoll.* 5.15; and, later than Iamblichus, in Julian's *Hymn to King Helios* 3.11, but nothing earlier that is extant, though it is presented as traditional. Snakes curling round his staff and facing each other is attested in *Schol. Thuc.* 1.53. If we take into account, however, the opening of the *De Mysteriis*—Θεὸς ὁ τῶν λόγων ἡγεμών, Ἑρμῆς, whom "Abammon" hails as "the common patron of all priests"—we may conclude that the Hermes being saluted here is the Egyptian Hermes (= Thoth) rather than the Greek, as he much more deserves the epithet *logios* than his Greek counterpart.

Lines 3–4. οἱ δεδοκιμασμένοι καὶ πρόκριτοι. The identity of these "proved and select" philosophers is not quite clear, but very probably the reference is to the early Pythagoreans and Platonists. The term πρόκριτος is taken ultimately from Athenian political terminology, according to which officials are selected ἐκ προκρίτων, "from a preselected list," terminology used by Plato at *Resp.* 7.537d and *Leg.* 12.945b. In the transferred sense used here by Iamblichus, however, it seems, strangely, to be used primarily by church fathers, to describe Peter among the apostles (ὁ πρόκριτος τῶν ἀποστόλων Πέτρος) or the apostles among other men, but Michael Psellus, much later, produces the phrase τῶν δ' Ἑλλήνων οἱ πρόκριτοι (*Omn. doctr.* 59,8). The linking with δεδοκιμασμένος, however, does not seem to be attested elsewhere.

Lines 4–5. ἡ τῶν Μουσῶν πρεσβυτάτη Καλλιόπη. Calliope, as eldest of the Muses, is traditionally associated with epic poetry, not dialectic, but what Iamblichus appears to be thinking of is a passage of Hesiod's *Theogony* (79–93), where Calliope is presented as endowing kings, in particular, with the gift of wise and persuasive speech, which Iamblichus could interpret as prowess in dialectical reasoning. The phrase αἰδοῖ μειλιχίῃ "with honey-sweet modesty" (line 92)—which also occurs in a similar passage from Homer, *Od.* 8.172—properly refers to the king so inspired, rather than Calliope herself, but that is no real problem.

Line 5. ἄπταιστον. This epithet is found also in *Myst.* 3.31.179 as a characteristic of truth.

Line 7. καθ' Ἡράκλειτον. A reference here to Heraclitus fragment B 93 Diels-Kranz, also quoted by Plutarch, *Pyth. orac.* 404E. The claim that Apollo, by reason of the ἀμφιβολία καὶ ὁμωνυμία associated with his prophecies, could be regarded as a stimulator of dialectical reasoning does not appear to be made elsewhere. Plutarch's point is the rather different one that Apollo makes use of the mortal body of the Delphic priestess to communicate wisdom to humankind, albeit in a diluted form.

Line 11. τὸ ξύλινον τεῖχος. This story is told originally by Herodotus 7.141–143, whence Iamblichus could well have taken it, but it is also mentioned by Plutarch in his *Them.* 10.2.

Line 12. ὁ ἐν Βραγχίδαις θεός. This is a reference to the oracle of Apollo at Didyma in Asia Minor, near Miletus, which was served by a guild of priests who were the notional descendants of a (probably mythical) Branchos, and thus Branchidae. Iamblichus makes mention of the Branchidae also at *Myst.* 3.11.123, there, as here, referring to the oracle, curiously, as if Branchidae were a place name rather than a class of persons, but this mode of reference in fact goes back to Herodotus (1.157; 5.36)—though he once (1.158) refers to οἱ Βραγχίδαι θεοπρόποι. As for the oracle, or utterance, this is couched in Ionic, but it does not occur in Herodotus. For Iamblichus, it seems to illustrate the procedure of ἐπαγωγή, instancing as it does an arrow, a lyre, and a ship, before generalizing to οὔτε ἄλλο οὐδέν.

Letter 6: *To Dyscolius, On Ruling* (?)

This letter lacks a topic in the manuscripts, but "ruling" certainly seems to be a suitable one, to judge by the contents. Also, its recipient, Dyscolius, may well be identical with a man who was governor of Syria in around 323 C.E. (*PLRE* 1:275), and as such this would be of particular relevance to him.

Iamblichus here is concerned to emphasize the theme of εὐεργεσία, or benefaction, which was certainly a salient aspect of public life in late antiquity. He seeks to emphasize the point that the true strength of an administrator is the happiness of those under his care, and this is where a sense of justice and fairness prevails, sweetened by regular distributions and entertainments and the sponsoring of public works. The principle that private advantage should not be separated from the public good is both good Platonism and good sense (see *Resp.* 5.462c–d: all citizens should share the same pleasures and pains, should call the same things "mine" and "not mine"). Iamblichus here asserts it as a general principle, true of all natural and social organisms. It is interesting, and no doubt a sign of the times, that the function of security is very much played down here—just a passing mention of σωτηρία as one of the purposes of good government—yet in Syria the Persians were always there as a threat.

The second fragment drives home the point by indulging in a veritable encomium of εὐεργεσία, emphasizing the aspect of unstintedness and open-handedness that it is desirable for a ruler to exhibit. All very well, a beleaguered governor might say, but this all depends on the level of revenue that one can bring in in the first place. Iamblichus says nothing about taxation here!

Fragment 1.2–3. χορηγίαν … σωτηρίαν … ῥαστώνην. This juxtaposition of three basic purposes of government—the provision of a comfortable level of material goods (though ἄπλετος seems a somewhat excessive epithet!), security from threats of violence both internal and external, and sufficient leisure for cultural activities—does not seem to occur elsewhere in this explicit form and constitutes a good summary of the purposes of government, in all ages.

Fragment 1.3. ζωῆς ῥαστώνην. The concept that leisure leads to the pursuit of philosophy is expressed by Aristotle at *Metaph.* A 982b23. Iamblichus is not here explicitly suggesting this as the result of leisure, but he may well have the passage in mind.

Fragment 1.6. οἱ ἐπιτρέψαντες αὐτῷ ἑαυτούς. This notion of rule as based on some kind of social contract is notable, since in fact there is no question of the citizenry of Syria having "entrusted themselves" to Roman rule.

Fragment 1.6–7. οὐ γὰρ δὴ κεχώρισται τὸ κοινὸν συμφέρον τοῦ ἰδίου. This sentiment may be seen as a variant on Socrates' remark in the *Republic* (7.519e) that "the object of legislation is not the welfare of any particular class but of the whole community."

Fragment 2.1. τὴν μεγαλοφροσύνην καὶ τὴν μεγαλοπρέπειαν. Both these nouns are Platonic (*Symp.* 194b; *Resp.* 6.486a), but they are not used together as synonyms. In Clement of Alexandria (*Strom.* 7.3), we find both nouns listed close together as species of courage (ἀνδρεία), but nowhere else do they seem to be linked in this way.

Fragment 2.3. ἀκριβολογῶνται. In Plato, this verb has only the positive connotation of "accuracy" (e.g., *Resp.* 1.340e; *Crat.* 415a), but in Aristotle, *Eth. nic.* 1127b8, we find ἀκριβολογία, in the sense of "petty reckoning of costs," as being inconsistent with μεγαλοπρέπεια.

Fragment 2.4. ὥσπερ ἐν πλάστιγγι ζυγοῦ. This expression is found in Plato, at *Resp.* 8.550e, in the course of the description of oligarchy, where the oligarchs are weighing wealth and goodness in a scale, to the detriment of goodness.

Fragment 2.5. ἐκ πίθου αὐτὰς προχέοντες. The image is used by Theocritus, in *Id.* 10.13: ἐκ πίθω ἀντλεῖς, where the scholiast ad loc. remarks that it is a proverbial expression; but it is hardly likely that Iamblichus derived it from that source. No other extant source suggests itself, however.

Letter 7: *To Eustathius, On Music*

This is a tiny fragment, and what remains to us has nothing obvious to do with μουσική. The context in which Stobaeus preserves it indicates that it should concern "training and education" (ἀγωγὴ καὶ παιδεία). Possibly a Pythagorean-influenced point is being made about the importance of μουσική in building character: without it, those with the greatest natural abilities will go to the bad most spectacularly.

Eustathius himself is an important figure in Iamblichus's circle, since, along with Aedesius, he was instrumental in moving the School to Pergamum after Iamblichus's death (in the early 320s) and then to his native Cappadocia. Much later, in 357, he is the recipient of a letter (*Letter 1*) from Basil of Caesarea, showing him at that time to be normally established at Caesarea in Cappadocia, though indulging in many travels, notably to Egypt and Persia. It is interesting that Basil, as a prominent Christian churchman, is corresponding amiably with the senior representative of Iamblichean Platonism. It is a testimony to the tact and civility of both men.

The sentiment expressed here, that great natures can produce great evils, is of course perfectly Platonic (see *Resp.* 6.491a–e).

Line 2. τὰ κράτιστα ἐπιτηδεύματα. How exactly to translate this phrase is something of a problem. Ἐπιτηδεύματα can mean anything like "pursuit," "business," "custom," or "habit," and κράτιστα "best, or "strongest." We have tried to express what is probably the dominant meaning. The sentiment seems to be based ultimately on a passage in *Leg.* 7.793de, where the Athenian Stranger utters a warning on the importance of preventing the infrastructure of the state, in the way of "laws, habits, or institutions" (νόμους ἢ ἔθη ... ἢ ἐπιτηδεύματα) from going askew, as that will bring the whole fabric of the state crashing down, like an insecurely constructed building.

Letter 8: To Macedonius, On Fate

This is undoubtedly the most philosophically substantial letter in the collection, and it merits close study, as the topic of Fate leads Iamblichus to give at least a sketch of his larger metaphysical system. The recipient, Macedonius, is unfortunately not otherwise known (unless he be the father of certain pupils of Libanius, see the introduction to this volume) but may be fairly safely assumed to have been a prominent member of the Syrian elite.

Iamblichus begins this epistolary treatise (the opening line, at any rate, sounds like a beginning) with a resounding assertion of the unity of creation as a whole, as a backdrop to his assertion of the unity of Fate as a concatenation of multifarious causes. We are presented with a relatively simple metaphysics, which disregards the complexities of the fully developed system revealed in Iamblichus's *Timaeus Commentary* and other works, consisting of a One, a level of primal Being (τὸ πρώτως ὄν), and a principle of Multiplicity (the Indefinite Dyad), which serves as a matrix for the system of Forms, presented here as causal principles (τὰ πολλὰ αἴτια), which come into being in Intellect (here presented as Being). The Forms constitute a coherent system, and it is on this analogy that Iamblichus wishes to present the multiplicity of causal sequences of the physical realm, which come together into one chain (εἷς εἱρμός) and so constitute a single "order" (τάξις), which is Fate (εἱμαρμένη).

This all so far presents a thoroughly Stoic aspect, according to which all things would seem to be ruled by Fate, but in fragment 2 Iamblichus introduces the soul as a principle that combines both an aspect that transcends the realm of generation and destruction over which Fate rules, thus enjoying a life of free will (ἡ αὐτεξούσιος ... ζωή), and an aspect that is subject to Fate by reason of its descent into embodied existence.

Iamblichus's doctrine of the soul is quite distinctive. It is presented by him in his *De anima* in opposition to that of his immediate predecessors Plotinus and Porphyry, in that he does not accept, as did Plotinus, that a part of the soul "remains above," but nonetheless he does not deny, as we see here, that the soul has a higher aspect, and when it is acting in accordance with that aspect of itself, it transcends fate. In fragment 3, indeed, he specifies that it is in accordance with this, or with our νοῦς, that we should live, and such a life will free us from the trammels of fate, which only prevail in the physical realm.

Even in this physical realm, he goes on to assert in fragment 4, the movements of fate are subordinated to "the good order [εὐταξία] of the intelligible and transcendent realm," which is providence (πρόνοια). But how, we may ask, does this impact on the issue of free will and necessity? Even the accomplished sage, after all, in so far as he is still in the body, is subject to the ineluctable laws of cause and effect. However, as a good Platonist, Iamblichus is concerned to assert the autonomy of the human will. It was a—slightly illogical but consistent—position in later Platonism (see Alcinous, *Did.* 26; Apuleius, *Dogm. Plat.* 1.12; Calcidius, *In Tim.* 142–190) that fate has the status of a law and operates hypothetically: that is to say, *if* you undertake a certain course of action, certain consequences will follow, but it is *up to us* (ἐφ' ἡμῖν) whether we initiate the given action (e.g., embark on sea voyage). This, as has often been pointed out, would not greatly impress a Stoic such as Chrysippus; after all, no enquiry is made into the question of the hidden causes and character traits that might impel one to undertake the given action in the first place. But it was a cornerstone of the Platonist position that at least the virtuous soul is autonomous—"Virtue owns no master," as Plato had asserted in *Resp.* 10.617e. As Iamblichus maintains, "the originating cause of action in humans has indeed a concordance with both these originating causes in the universe (sc. fate and providence), but it is also the case that the origin of action in us is independent of Nature and emancipated from the movement of the universe. For this reason it is not implicated in the originative principle of the universe."

Iamblichus goes on, in fragments 5–7, to deal with a major objection to the concept of the providential ordering of sublunar affairs, the phenomenon of chance occurrences (ταὐτόματον καὶ ἡ τύχη, frg. 5.1) and the unequal apportionments of fortune that result from this (παρ' ἀξίαν αἱ διανομαί, frg. 6.1). His response to this objection is robust. It is simply wrong to assume that there are any arbitrary breaks in the causal sequence. Chance is to be defined as the "overseer and connecting cause" (ἔφορος καὶ συναγωγὸς αἰτία, frg. 5.7) of a multiplicity of causal chains, which presides over them, sometimes as a god, sometimes as a daemon.

Iamblichus is less than clear here, though he is operating within the parameters of traditional Platonic doctrine. Chance and unequal apportionments of good fortune were indeed a problem for the doctrine of divine providence, but Platonists would maintain that if, for example, you were passing beneath a building while in pursuit of some rational objective and a large piece of masonry fell off the building and killed you, that was simply the result of the operation of a plurality of causal chains, the conjunction of which was somehow necessary to the administration of the cosmos as a whole. Further, Iamblichus would claim that the virtuous or wise man will regard such events as he cannot control by his own will and prudent decision-making as unimportant and not impinging on his happiness (frg. 7).

In fact, his position in all this is thoroughly Stoic in tendency and very little different from that of Plotinus, as a comparison with *Enn.* 3.1 [3] *On Fate* and 3.2–3 [47–48] *On Providence* will show, but particularly the former, which is an early essay and quite traditional (see esp. chs. 7–10, where the Platonist position is presented). While there are no precise verbal echoes, the doctrine is very similar.

Fragment 1.1. Πάντα μὲν τὰ ὄντα τῷ ἑνί ἐστιν ὄντα. This principle may be compared with the beginning of Plotinus, *Enn.* 6.9.1–2, of which this is a direct quotation, but it can be traced back to Aristotle, *Metaph.* 1054a13–19. It may well constitute the beginning of the letter, even as the same statement opens Plotinus's tractate.

Fragment 1.3. κατὰ μίαν συμπλοκήν. This phrase, employed widely by later Platonists (e.g., Plotinus, *Enn.* 3.1.4), serves to express the principle of the universal coherence of causes that is basic to Iamblichus's position here. At *Enn.* 3.1.2.30, we may note, Plotinus also uses the phrase τὴν τῶν αἰτίων ἐπιπλοκήν (in conjunction with τὸν ἄνωθεν εἱρμόν).

Fragment 1.5. πολυειδῶν ὄντων καὶ πολυμερίστων. This combination of adjectives is notable. The former is common enough, but the latter is unattested elsewhere except in a scholiast on Oppian, *Hal.* 4.409. It is used again by Iamblichus in *Letter* 10.2.6 below.

Fragment 1.9. οὗτος τοίνυν εἷς εἱρμός. We have here a key statement of Iamblichus's doctrine, in accordance with which the whole multiplicity of phenomena may be traced back to a single principle governing all sublunary life, which he describes just below as a τάξις comprehending within itself all other τάξεις, that is to say, causal chains or structures. The use of εἱρμός in connection with fate is to be found in Plotinus's essay *On Fate* (*Enn.* 3.1.2.31 and 4.11), but the definition of fate as μία τάξις πάσας τάξεις ὁμοῦ περιλαβοῦσα ἐν αὑτῇ (lines 13–14) does not occur there.

Fragment 2.1. Οὐσία ἐστὶν ἄϋλος ἡ τῆς ψυχῆς καθ᾽ ἑαυτήν. The term ἄϋλος is first attested in Aristotle (*Gen. corr.* 322a28), but the following three—ἀσώματος, ἀγέννητος, ἀνώλεθρος—take their origin from Plato himself, the latter two being found conjoined at *Tim.* 52a.

Fragment 2.4-5. τὴν αὐτεξούσιον καὶ τὴν ἀπόλυτον περιείληφεν ἐν ἑαυτῇ ζωήν. Plotinus uses αὐτεξούσιος only rarely as an adjective (as opposed to τὸ αὐτεξούσιον, used as a noun), but he does so at *Enn.* 6.8.20.32: αὐτεξουσίῳ, referring to God's power, with ἀπόλυτος occurring earlier in the same chapter, also referring to God: ἀπόλυτον τὴν ποίησις αὐτοῦ τιθημένοις. Iamblichus uses αὐτεξούσιος also three times in the *De mysteriis* (3.14, 17, 23), to refer to a certain type of divination that is imparted to us voluntarily by the gods; and ἀπόλυτος of the hypercosmic soul at *In Tim.* frg. 50,20 Dillon.

Fragment 3.2. τὴν ἀδέσποτον τῆς ψυχῆς ἐξουσίαν. This phrase embodies a reminiscence of *Resp.* 10.617e: ἀρετὴ δ᾽ ἀδέσποτος.

Fragment 3.3-4. οὐκ ἀνθρώπινόν τινα βίον, ἀλλὰ τὸν θεῖον. For this thought, see Plotinus, *Enn.* 1.2.6.1-2: "our concern is not merely to be sinless, but to be gods."

Fragment 4.1. Καὶ γὰρ ἤδη τὸ ὅλον εἰπεῖν. This whole paragraph is devoted to driving home the theme of the comprehensive dependence of εἱμαρμένη on πρόνοια, in a way that, if anything, sets εἱμαρμένη in a rather positive light. All the activities of fate in the sublunar realm are modeled on archetypes in the intelligible realm, and, finally, its very οὐσία is entwined with that of providence. Fate is not, thus, so much a deviation from divine providence as a necessary projection of it.

Fragment 4.9. Τούτων δ' οὕτως ἐχόντων. The position of the human soul (or "originating cause of action") is specified here as constituting a bridge between these two realms, and having a συμφωνία with each of them, while being itself essentially free from the domination of Nature and the power of the physical world. In this connection, it seems necessary to insert <ἡ> before ἐν ἡμῖν (line 12), as this phrase needs to be subject rather than predicate of the sentence preceding it.

Fragment 4.18-19. λόγον καθαρὸν αὐθυπόστατον καὶ αὐτοκίνητον. The essence of this pure λόγος that the soul contains within itself is comprised in the terms αὐθυπόστατος and αὐτοκίνητος, the latter of which occurs first in Aristotle (*Phys.* 258a2)—though the concept goes back to Plato, *Phdr.* 245c7: τὸ αὐτὸ κινοῦν—but the former of which appears to be a coinage of Iamblichus himself, to characterize an essential feature of each of the principal hypostases, that it constitutes itself at the culmination of its outflow from its prior. See John Whittaker, "The Historical Background of Proclus' Doctrine of the *Authupostata*," in *De Jamblique à Proclus: Neuf exposés suivis de discussions* (Entretiens sur l'antiquité classique 21; Geneva: Fondation Hardt, 1975), 193-237. The concept, without the term, is actually expressed by Porphyry at *Sent.* 17: "The soul is an essence without magnitude, immaterial and indestructible, which has come to exist in a state of life that holds its living from itself [παρ' ἑαυτῆς]"—itself distilled, in all probability, from such a passage as Plotinus, *Enn.* 4.7.9.

Fragment 5.7-8. τότε μὲν θεὸν ἐπικαλοῦμεν. The distinction made here between "god" and "daemon" (the latter a certain supplement to the text, in view of what follows) is peculiar, but Iamblichus seems to be saying that, if chance is directed by supernatural causes, we must postulate a higher level of divinity as directing it than if it is directed by purely natural causes. This distinction may possibly arise from an Homeric ἀπορία generated by the fact that Homer sometimes attributes accidental happenings to a θεός but at other times to a δαίμων. Porphyry may well have dealt with such an ἀπορία in his *Homerika Zétémata*, but we have unfortunately no record of that.

Fragment 6.8. ἡ τῆς ψυχῆς ἀκρότης καὶ τελειότης. This conjunction of terms for the highest part of the soul is interesting. Both of these terms are frequently used elsewhere by Iamblichus, as they are later by Proclus, but not in conjunction, as they have rather different connotations.

LETTER 9: TO MACEDONIUS, ON CONCORD

The topic of concord, ὁμόνοια, has a long history in political discourse. It is first attested in the mid-fifth century B.C.E., when it tends to become a catchword, predominantly in conservative circles, for the sort of ideal political situation resulting from the lower classes knowing their place and agreeing to be ruled by their betters. We have preserved to us a fragment of a significant address (85B1 Diels-Kranz) delivered to an aristocratic political club, probably in the 420s, by the sophist Thrasymachus, in which he says that, "instead of concord [ὁμόνοια], we have reached a state of mutual hostility and chaos," and laments the good old days of the "ancestral constitution." Significant also is the treatise on ὁμόνοια composed by the Athenian sophist and reactionary politician Antiphon, though the surviving fragments are curiously unhelpful in ascertaining what the main thrust of the work was (fragments assembled and translated in John M. Dillon and Tania Gergel, eds., *The Greek Sophists* [London: Penguin, 2003], 158–66, with comments ad loc.). There is also the interesting report in Thucydides (8.93.3), in the context of the crisis arising from the coup by the Four Hundred in Athens in 411, that the conservative leaders invited the democrats in the Piraeus to an assembly to discuss ὁμόνοια. This in fact resulted in the decommissioning of the Four Hundred and the establishment (albeit briefly) of the Five Thousand, which Thucydides, himself of moderately conservative views, characterizes as "the best regime that the Athenians ever enjoyed within my memory" (8.97).

This connotation, of the voluntary submission of the lower orders, who would tend to be ruled by their passions, to rule by their betters, who would be naturally infused with rationality, is equally applicable in the later Roman Empire, and if Macedonius is, as we conjecture, an imperial administrator, this is most aptly addressed to him. Iamblichus adds a Platonic dimension to the argument by applying the concept of ὁμόνοια also to the individual, specifying that it is above all the rational soul that is at one with itself, while it is that soul which is subject to its passions that is liable to be at odds with itself (διχογνωμονῶν πρὸς ἑαυτόν, line 7). It is interesting that it is not here explicitly stated that the contrast is between reason and the passions, but, from a Platonist point of view, there is no question of a rational individual being "in two minds"; that is a sign of irrationality and the pull of opposite desires.

Line 1. καθάπερ αὐτὸ τὸ ὄνομα βούλεται ἐνδείκνυσθαι. This "etymology" is appropriate primarily to the individual, since it involves the ὁμοιότης of a single νοῦς.

Line 2. ὁμοίου τοῦ νοῦ. This is a curious, but possible, use of ὅμοιος in the sense of "similar to itself." We have chosen to render this "well-balanced."

Line 5. ὁμογνωμοσύνην. This is a rare word, attested, for example, in Josephus, *C. Ap.* 2.270.

Line 7. διχογνωμονῶν. Apart from an isolated usage in Xenophon (*Mem.* 2.6.21), this is a rare word, attested, for example, in Dio Cassius, *Hist.* 43.16 and 44.25. See also Libanius, *Decl.* 43.43.

Lines 8–9. ὁμοφροσύνης ἐστὶ πλήρης. The word ὁμοφροσύνη is rare and poetical enough to allow one to suspect that Iamblichus is here summoning up a reminiscence of the famous passage in *Od.* 6 (181–182), where Odysseus is addressing Nausicaa, praising her and calling down blessings upon her: καὶ ὁμοφροσύνην ὀπάσειαν (sc. οἱ θεοί) / ἐσθλήν.

Letter 10. To Olympius, On Courage

Concerning the addressee, we know of an Olympius who was the father of a pupil of Libanius (*Ep.* 539), who became a doctor in Antioch, but was also skilled in grammar and philosophy. This identification would fit chronologically and geographically but must remain no more than a probability.

Courage, ἀνδρεία, is the most troublesome virtue to deal with from a philosophical point of view, since, in the vulgar acceptance of the term, it can be possessed in a high degree by individuals who might have little claim to any of the other three canonical virtues: wisdom, moderation, and justice. It becomes necessary, therefore, for a Platonist to redefine courage rather radically before it can fit comfortably with the others. The process begins already in Plato's *Laches,* where Socrates, at 199a, takes on board the definition of courage attempted by Nicias at 195a, "Knowledge of what is to be feared and hoped for in war and all other situations," and in effect generalizes it, to make it coextensive with virtue in general (199e). More immediately, however, Iamblichus is probably influenced also by the Stoic definition of courage as "knowledge of what is and is not worthy to be feared" (e.g., *SVF* 3.262)

Iamblichus here, particularly in fragment 1, continues in this tradition, following most immediately Plotinus, in such a passage as *Enn.* 1.2.3, where Plotinus identifies courage at the purificatory level with "not being afraid to depart from the body." Porphyry also, in *Sent.* 32, provides definitions of courage at the "higher" levels of virtue that have relevance to Iamblichus's exposition here. At lines 55–56, we learn that courage at the intellective level consists in "detachment from the passions, through which the soul assimilates itself to that towards which it turns its gaze," and at 65–66, courage at the "paradigmatic" level of virtue is defined simply as "self-identity" (ταυτότης).

We must note, though, that there is no indication, in what survives of this letter, that Iamblichus is making any distinction between levels of virtue, though we know him, in his treatise *On the Virtues,* to have gone even beyond his immediate predecessors in proposing fully seven levels of virtue (apud Damascius, *In Phaed.* 113,14–25. Norvin). Such elaborations, however, would not be appropriate in a work of popular philosophy. In the second fragment, indeed, he is primarily concerned with courage at what Plotinus would have described as the "civic" level.

Fragment 1.1. ἄτρεπτος νοερὰ δύναμις. This sets the tone for the first fragment. The adjective ἄτρεπτος seems to be first attested in Stoic circles, being used (probably) by Chrysippus at *SVF* 2.482 (from Diogenes Laertius 7.150), but also by Pseudo-Aristotle, *Mund.* 401b19. It is notable that, comparing *Myst.* 2.9.88, Iamblichus gives as the result of the invocation of archangels ἄχραντον κατάστασιν νοερὰν τε θεωρίαν καὶ δύναμιν ἄτρεπτον, all of which should be interpreted as the "higher" ἀνδρεία.

Fragment 1.2. τοῦ νοῦ ταυτότης. This is a particularly interesting formulation, in view of Porphyry's definition of courage at the "paradigmatic" level (*Sent.* 32.69) as ταυτότης, "self-identity," presumably in the sense of "unwaveringness." This definition of Porphyry's, in turn, bears an interesting relation to Plotinus's definition at *Enn.* 1.2.7.5–6, where the manuscripts read ἀϋλότης, "immateriality," which seems rather weak in the context but where the real reading may be a term that Plotinus would have concocted for the purpose, αὐτότης, "selfness," which Porphyry would be here "toning down" somewhat. At all events, Iamblichus seems here to be directly dependent on Porphyry rather than Plotinus.

Fragment 2.1. περί τε δεινὰ καὶ μὴ δεινά. We have here an echo of the basic Stoic definition of the virtue of courage, as noted above.

Fragment 2.6. πολυμέριστα εἴδη τῆς ἀνδρείας. For the rare adjective πολυμέριστος (for the more usual πολυμερής), see above on *Letter* 8, frg. 1.5.

Fragment 2.7. ἀήττητος πάντῃ καὶ ἀβίαστος. For ἀήττητος, see Plato, *Resp.* 2.375a, where θυμός is said to make the soul ἄφοβός τε καὶ ἀήττητος. Ἀβίαστος is also Platonic (*Tim.* 61a).

Fragment 2.10. καὶ θαρροῦσα τὸν θάνατον καὶ μελετῶσα. A reference here to the Platonic doctrine that the philosopher should "practice dying" (*Phd.* 67e).

Letter 11: *To Poemenius, On Fate* (?)

This fragment is not equal in significance to the earlier treatise to Macedonius, but it contains some aspects of interest nonetheless. Fate is presented here in very much the same terms as providence, as being a benign force in the world, directed by the gods, whereas in the *Letter to Macedonius* it comes across as more of an autonomous force in the Stoic mode, though still of positive tendency overall. Indeed, having first used the alternative term for fate, πεπρωμένη (line 5), Iamblichus, in the last part of the fragment, speaks of "providence," πρόνοια (line 8), though in the context of fate's preserving both its goodness and human freedom—an interesting, if rather fuzzy, assertion. This all makes it less than certain that, despite the mention of fate in the first line, this letter is really about fate rather than providence. It may very well be that Iamblichus is simply concerned to assert that gods direct fate for the best and that his topic is really providence. Note, however, that he is also anxious to assert the autonomy (αὐτεξούσιον) of the human soul alongside the workings of divine providence (see *Letter* 8.2.4).

Lines 1–2. ἡ δ' ἐπανόρθωσις αὐτῶν. This assertion of the gods' "sound direction" or "corrective action" as a feature of fate finds no parallel in *Letter* 8 above, nor yet in *Letter* 12. It is an indication of a more "theological" tone to this letter.

Line 5. σῴζεται ἡ πεπρωμένη. We find the terms εἱμαρμένη and πεπρωμένη linked also at *Vit. Pyth.* 32.219.

Lines 7–8. εἰς τὴν ἄτακτον πλημμέλειαν. A reminiscence, perhaps, of Plato, *Tim.* 30a, where the precosmic Receptacle is said to move πλημμελῶς καὶ ἀτάκτως. Certainly there are many reminiscences of this phrase in *De mysteriis*, such as 1.10.36; 1.18.54; 3.3.108; 3.25.158.

LETTER 12: *TO SOPATER, ON FATE*

Whatever may be said about the previous passage, this fragment—the first of a series directed to Iamblichus's chief pupil Sopater of Apamea (ca. 270–330 C.E.)—is clearly about fate and concords broadly with the contents of the *Letter to Macedonius*. Fate here is portrayed as inherent in Nature, which Iamblichus characterizes as the "immanent causal principle" (ἀχώριστος αἰτία, line 2) of the universe, holding the whole material world together in an ineluctable sequence of cause and effect. This places Fate definitively at the encosmic level of reality, which is something that our higher soul can transcend (even though Iamblichus does not accept the Plotinian doctrine of an "undescended" level of soul). The "higher essences and orders" (αἱ κρείττονες οὐσίαι καὶ διακοσμήσεις, line 3) that preside over this causal sequence transcendentally (χωριστῶς, line 3) will presumably be the supracosmic levels of divinity, in particular the demiurgic level of gods (but Iamblichus is not concerned here to be specific).

The long list of parallel phrases comprising the last sentence is a characteristic example of Iamblichean prose.

We may note that Sopater himself is credited with a work *On Providence, and On Those Who Fare Well or Ill Contrary to Their Deserts* (περὶ προνοίας καὶ τῶν παρὰ τὴν ἀξίαν εὐπραγούντων ἢ δυσπραγούντων, Suda, s.v. Sopatros).

Line 4. λόγος γενεσιουργός. The adjective occurs frequently in Iamblichus, as in *Myst.* 1.11; 2.7; *Vit. Pyth.* 32.228 (and see γενεσιουργία in *Comm. math.* 41,28 and 92,21 Festa).

LETTER 13: *TO SOPATER, ON DIALECTIC*

This letter may be compared with that to another pupil, Dexippus (*Letter 5* above), but it is couched in much more sober terms. Nonetheless, dialectic receives high praise here, too; the reference to its being "a gift of the gods" (τὸ τῶν θεῶν δῶρον, line 3 of frg. 1) may be taken as a reminiscence of *Phileb.* 16c: θεῶν εἰς ἀνθρώπους δόσις. In the *Letter to Dexippus* it is credited either to the god Hermes or to "the eldest of the Muses," Calliope. Its usefulness as a preliminary to all forms of rational discourse is emphasized by the distinction of four levels of such discourse: (1) ordinary conversation (ἐντεύξεις, line 6), which employs κοιναὶ ἐννοίαι and δόξαι (line 6); (2) scientific enquiry (εὑρέσεις τῶν τέχνων, line 7), when one is seeking out the first principles of a given τέχνη; (3) practical deliberation (λογιζόμενον, line 8), prior to taking action; and, lastly, (4) preliminary exercises (προγυμνασία, line 8) prior to embarking on philosophical enquiry.

The second fragment here is quoted by Stobaeus directly after the first, and indeed it is not clear that there is any gap between them. It may be that he divided them more for aesthetic reasons than anything else, to highlight the specific discussion of the usefulness of dialectic for philosophy. Notable here are the references to Socrates' quizzing of Meno's slave boy in the *Meno* (82b–84a), leading to recollection (ἀνάμνησις) and to Socrates' practice of "midwifery" in the *Theaetetus* (see 150d; 210c), leading to the discernment of whether a given conception is true and valid or a mere "wind-egg"—both exercises of dialectic.

Fragment 1.5. χρησιμώτατον ... διαφερόντως. Wachsmuth here calls attention to the usage of διαφερόντως with a superlative in the *De mysteriis* (3.1.102: διαφερόντως κοινοτάτη) as a possibly Iamblichean peculiarity. See also *Protr.* 98,18 Pistelli: ἐγκρατέστατον ... διαφερόντως.

Fragment 1.8. προγυμνασία. This is a rare word, attested previously only in Philo, *Mos.* 1.60 (conjoined with μελέτη).

Fragment 1.23. τὸ ἐν Πυθοῖ γράμμα. The well-known injunction allegedly carved on the portal of Apollo's temple at Delphi, γνῶθι σεαυτόν ("Know thyself"). See the reference in the *Letter to Dexippus* to the God of Delphi stirring up his auditors to dialectical enquiry by, in Heraclitus's words "not speaking out, nor yet concealing, but signifying."

Fragment 2.2–3. <ὥς> καὶ ὁ Σωκράτης ἐπιδεικνύει ἐν τῷ Μένωνι. This seems to be a rather general remark on the content of the *Meno*. Socrates, however, emphasizes that he is not teaching but simply triggering recollection by questioning somebody. See *Men.* 84c–d.

Fragment 2.4. αἱ μαιείας ἕνεκα προσαγόμεναι. This seems to refer to such a passage as *Theaet.* 150a–c, where Socrates explains his procedure of dialectical "midwifery."

LETTER 14: TO SOPATER, ON BRINGING UP CHILDREN

Sopater was in fact a family man—we know of two sons, Sopater the Younger and Himerius (the latter of whom had a son named Iamblichus)—so this letter is suitably addressed to him. The letter begins with a clear reference to Plato's *Laws* (6.765e), where the Stranger says, à propos the role of the Minister of Education in Magnesia: "Any living creature that flourishes in its first stages of growth gets a tremendous impetus towards its natural perfection and the final development appropriate to it, and this is true of both plants and animals, tame and wild, and men too" (trans. Saunders). This places Iamblichus's theory of education firmly within Platonic parameters, as of course one would expect. This continues in the section that follows, with the emphasis on good example from parents (as well as tutors and teachers), accompanied by the training of the children's sensibilities, teaching them to "love and hate the right things" (see *Leg.* 2.653a–b). All this borrows much from Plato's discussion of education in books 1, 2, and 7 of the *Laws*.

A strong distinction is made, as indeed is made in the *Laws*, between the prerational and rational stages of education, but Iamblichus is more explicit about the ultimate end of education, which is to lead up the young person, by easy stages, to an understanding of the (First) Cause—simply referred to as ἡ αἰτία—which bestows validation and certainty upon the definitions of the virtues that precede it. Iamblichus makes a good point about not laying arguments that require a full measure of scientific discernment (εὐκρίνεια ἐπιστημονική, line 33) upon minds not mature enough to comprehend them, but even that is implicit in Plato's program in *Laws* 7.

It is worth remarking, perhaps, that both of Sopater's sons seem to have been a credit to him, Sopater the Younger being prominent in the civic life of Apamea (he held the office of decurion), and Himerius holding various public offices in the imperial administration (Libanius, *Ep.* 573).

Line 6. ἐν ἁπαλαῖς ἔτι καὶ ἀβάτοις ψυχαῖς. The phraseology here is borrowed from *Phdr.* 245a: ἁπαλὴν καὶ ἄβατον ψυχήν.

Line 13. συμφωνίαν ἡδονῆς καὶ λύπης. A further reference to *Leg.* 2.653a–b.

Line 33. δι' εὐκρινείας ἐπιστημονικῆς. The term εὐκρίνεια, in this sense, seems to occur first in the Platonic *Definitions* (414a): εὐπορία εὐκρίνεια κρατητικὴ τοῦ λεγομένου. This injunction could be taken as an intimation of what Iamblichus himself is doing in the *Letters*.

Letter 15: To Sopater, On Ingratitude

The term ἀχαριστία (line 1) in the sense of "ingratitude" is not Platonic, though it is classical (e.g., Xenophon, *Cyr.* 1.2.7: Demosthenes 18.316). Plato does, however, use the word at *Resp.* 3.411e (with ἀρρυθμία), in the sense of "gracelessness." The sentiments here expressed have a special resonance in the context of the late Roman Empire, by reason of the culture of public and private beneficence that was then prevalent, calling for due gratitude to the noble benefactor both by municipalities and by individuals; but of course Iamblichus's exhortations here, being very general in nature, have a wider application. It could even be the case that he has in mind ingratitude in the face of divine beneficence (see below, note on lines 4–5).

Lines 4–5. τὸ κοινὸν τῆς θείας βοηθείας πάσης. There is indeed, as Meineke discerned, something somewhat peculiar about θείας in this context, though it could be given a meaning, if one supposed that Iamblichus were talking about ingratitude toward the gods. But this he does not seem to be doing, so in fact the θείας could be simply a sort of anticipatory dittography from βοηθείας, and κοινόν would then mean just "the commonwealth," as is indeed its more natural meaning, rather than "the world in general."

Line 5. πάνδεινον. This would seem to be a Platonic echo, inspired by *Resp.* 10.610d: πάνδεινον ἡ ἀδικία.

Line 7. τὰς μείζονας εὐποιΐας. The word εὐποιΐα is relatively late and has an interesting provenance, occurring first in the Epistle to the Hebrews (13:16): τῆς δὲ εὐποιΐας καὶ κοινωνίας μὴ ἐπιλανθάνεσθε· τοιαύταις γὰρ θυσίαις εὐαρεστεῖται ὁ θεός.

LETTER 16: TO SOPATER, ON VIRTUE

We have had a series of letters in the collection on the individual virtues: justice (to Anatolius); self-control (to Arete); (practical) wisdom (to Asphalius); and courage (to Olympius); and now we have a more comprehensive essay on virtue in general, to Iamblichus's favorite pupil.

The characterization of virtue as the τελειότης καὶ εὐμετρία (frg. 1.1) of the soul is notable only for the fact that the latter term is extremely rare. This is followed by a very Iamblichean sequence of epithets for the ἔργα of virtue, all of which, however, are fairly banal.

In the second fragment, a more distinctive theory emerges. Virtue is now presented almost in the role of the Form of the Good, and this tone is continued also in fragment 3. It emerges that its essence can only be contemplated by an intellect purified from all earthly influences and concerns. The three entities presented in the *Philebus* (65a–b) as being at the threshold of the Good—Beauty, Symmetry, and Truth—as well as a list of other attributes of the realm of True Being, are applied to it, and it is then spoken of as an intelligible Form (νοητὸν εἶδος, frg. 2.7). It all adds up to a distinctly otherworldly concept of virtue, equating not to the "civic" level of virtue in the Plotinian (and later Neoplatonic) schema but rather to the one of the higher levels: the purificatory, or perhaps even the paradigmatic.

Fragment 1.1. Ψυχῆς ... τελειότης καὶ εὐμετρία. See Democritus B 187 Diels-Kranz: ψυχῆς τελεότης. We found τελειότης earlier, used of the soul (*Letter* 8, frg. 6.8), combined—unusually—with ἀκρότης. As for εὐμετρία, it seems to occur before Iamblichus only in the medical writer Aretaeus (first century C.E.), *Cur. acut.* 23.

Fragment 1.2–3. τὰ δ' ἔργα τῆς ἀρετῆς. We find here a very characteristic Iamblichean list of epithets. None are particularly notable in themselves, though εὐκαιρία (frg. 1.4) may be borrowed from *Phdr.* 272a. It is not, however, a particularly rare word.

Fragment 2.1–2. ἀπολυομένου πάσης σωματοειδοῦς διαμορφώσεως. This characterization of virtue involves a rather notable phrase. Σωματοειδής occurs at *Phd.* 81b–c, 83d, and 86a, but διαμόρφωσις does not seem to occur before Plutarch (*An. procr.* 1023C), to describe the "shaping" of Matter by God.

Fragment 2.3. ταυτότης τε ἀμετάστατος. This is a distinctly Platonic/Platonist turn of phrase, indicating Iamblichus's assimilation of virtue to the intelligible realm.

Fragment 2.6. ἰδὲ ἅπαντα τὰ τοιαῦτα ἔνδειγμα. We are inclined to accept here the ingenious emendation of Rhode for the more or less meaningless manuscript reading εἰ δὲ ἅπαντα τὰ τοιαῦτα, ἓν δεῖγμα, which would have to be translated "If all these are such, one sufficient indication of it is provided." Paleographically, the emendation is easy and gives a much superior sense, even if the use of ἰδέ is somewhat odd, as being generally poetical (see, e.g., Euripides, *Or.* 1541, but also cf. *Phd.* 72a.). Iamblichus uses ἔνδειγμα, we may note, at *Myst.* 1.11.39.

Fragment 2.8. ἀμερίστως μεριζόμενον. There is something of an analogy to this at *Myst.* 1.9.31, where the "single, indivisible light of the gods" is described as being present indivisibly (ἀμερίστως) to all things that are capable of participating in it.

Fragment 2. 8. πληθυομένων. For the use of this term, see *Myst.* 1.6.19, where "the class of daemons" is described as being "multiplied in unity" (ἐν τῷ ἑνὶ πληθυόμενον).

Fragment 2.9. τῶν μεταλαμβανόντων. In the *Parmenides* (130e–131a), Plato discusses the consequences of partaking in Ideas such as Justice, using the same vocabulary.

Fragment 2.14. συμφερόμενον. Hense and Rhode's conjectures are certainly worth thinking about, but nevertheless to us they seem to be unnecessary.

Fragment 2.18. διακοσμεῖ τοῖς καλλίστοις δώροις. We are inclined to adopt the emendation of Thomas, δώροις, for the manuscript ὅροις, as making better sense, but "adorning with bounds or limits" is not impossible.

Fragment 3.1. κατὰ τὸν χωριστὸν νοῦν. Since Iamblichus does not believe in an undescended soul in the Plotinian sense, it seems more natural to take this as a reference to the cosmic Intellect. The distinction between a χωριστός and an ἀχώριστος νοῦς is found in Iamblichus's *Commentary on the Timaeus*, frg. 56 Dillon, in a comment on *Tim.* 36c, where the reference is to the World Soul and a cosmic Intellect. At all events, this is in line with Iamblichus's presentation of virtue as something that draws us away from worldly or material concerns.

Fragment 4.2. ἐξῃρημένος. Wyttenbach's and Wakefield's emendation seems necessary; ἐξῃρημένος is a common term in Iamblichean metaphysics; see *In Soph.* frg. 1,19 Dillon; *In Tim.* frg. 50,19 and 52,6 Dillon; *In Parm.* frg. 6,19 Dillon.

Letter 17: To Sopater, On Self-Respect

This passage is presented by Stobaeus in a section concerning αἰδώς and headed περὶ αἰδοῦς, but Hense is nonetheless inclined to take it as forming part of the letter *On Virtue*. We see no reason for this, as the tone, such as it is, exhibits none of the otherworldliness noticeable in that epistle. It is indeed quite banal in its content, though exhibiting a degree of rhetorical balance in its style. Indeed, it has the appearance of a peroration and probably forms the end of the letter from which it is taken.

There are a number of mentions of αἰδώς elsewhere in the Iamblichean corpus, but by no means all are relevant. At *Vit. Pyth.* 31.188, though, we are told that sincere respect (ἀνυπόκριτος αἰδώς) toward the elderly is one of the features of σωφροσύνη that Pythagoras sought to inculcate; in 33.233, a feature of Pythagorean friendship is stated to be that a relationship is formed "not carelessly and at random but with respect [μετ' αἰδοῦς], deep thought, and right order." At *In Nic.* 33,11, we find αἰδώς presented as the mean between κατάπληξις, "bashfulness," and ἀναισχυντία, "shamelessness." All these sentiments might well have found their way into a letter on self-respect.

Line 2. ἐξορίζοντα. The construction of this verb with the genitive without preposition is attested in Julian, *Or.* 6.186b. In Aristotle's *Pol.* 1336b15 we find it stated that the law-makers should banish (ἐξορίζειν) λόγοι ἀσχήμονες from the city. The verb also occurs in *Letter* 3.3, above.

LETTER 18: *To Sopater, On Truth*

The surviving fragment of this letter is concerned, not so much with commending truth in itself, but with contrasting it with appearance, to which Iamblichus, borrowing the term from Plato's *Soph.* 267e, gives the name of δοξομιμητικὴ εἰδωλοποιία (line 2). This strong contrast between the supra-cosmic, divine world as the proper province of truth, as opposed to the appearance that dominates the physical cosmos, calls to mind Iamblichus's attested exegesis of the *Sophist* (*In Soph.* frg. 1 Dillon), according to which the sophist portrayed in that dialogue is the sublunary demiurge, "image-maker and purifier of souls" (εἰδωλοποιὸς καὶ καθαρτὴς ψυχῶν), who is "bound up with nonbeing, engaged in the creation of material things, and embraces the 'true lie'"—while, however, directing his gaze toward True Being (τὸ ὄντως ὄν), even as Truth here concerns itself with τὰ ὄντως ὄντα.

Line 1. ὥσπερ καὶ τοὔνομα δηλοῖ. This seems to betoken an "etymology" of ἀλήθεια as something that "wanders" (ἀλᾶται) around divinities (περὶ θεούς), recalling the etymology in the *Cratylus*: θεία οὖσα ἄλη (421b). This would not be the only such "etymology" in the *Letters*; see that of ὁμόνοια in *Letter* 9.

Line 3. τὸ ἄθεον καὶ σκοτεινόν. This phrase is borrowed from Plato, *Alc.* 1.134e: εἰς τὸ ἄθεον καὶ σκοτεινὸν βλέποντες.

Line 4. νοητικοῖς. Probably one should read νοητοῖς here, but νοητικοῖς is not impossible, and the meaning is hardly affected.

Line 5. τὸ ἀνείδεον. The adjective occurs relatively late; see Plotinus, *Enn.* 1.8.3.14, as an epithet of Matter.

Line 6. ἀμβλυώττει. The verb is Platonic; see *Resp.* 6.508c6 and 7.516e9.

Line7. ὑποδύεται. On the meaning of this verb, see Plato, *Gorg.* 464c (used of flattery), and Aristotle, *Metaph.* 1004b18: οἱ γὰρ διαλεκτικοὶ καὶ σοφισταὶ τὸ αὐτὸ μὲν ὑποδύονται σχῆμα τῷ φιλοσόφῳ.

Line 7. πρόσχημα. This word is used in a positive sense at *Resp.* 6.495d: καλῶν δὲ ὀνομάτων καὶ προσχημάτων μεστήν; see also *Hipp. maj.* 286a–b. However, it also has a negative sense, as at *Prot.* 316d and 317a, where it is used of a pretense put up by sophists.

Line 8. θηρεύεται. A further reference to the *Sophist*, 222a. There the sophist is described as a hunter who later on in the same dialogue is portrayed as the deceiving sorcerer and deceptive creator of false imitations (232b–237b).

Line 9. ἐξαπατᾷ. Deception is something that the Divine (with which Truth is here associated) does not indulge in; see *Resp.* 2.382e: οὔτε αὐτὸς (sc. ὁ θεός) μεθίσταται οὔτε ἄλλους ἐξαπατᾷ.

Letter 19: To an Unknown Recipient, On Marriage

This short extract, to an unidentified recipient—who might indeed be Sopater—seems to embody a principle derived from Aristotle's *Politics*, that the rule of husband over wife is akin to that exercised by constitutional rulers over citizens in a πόλις.

In Aristotle's *Politics* (1254b13-15), the male sex is stronger by nature (φύσει) and therefore rules (τὸ ἄρχον) by nature (cf. line 1). The female sex is weaker and is therefore ruled (τὸ ἀρχόμενον). In 1252a24-27 Aristotle points out that there are three different kinds of relationships in a given household: between husband and wife; between father and child; and between master and slave. In all of these relationships, the head of the household is the authoritative figure for Aristotle. Yet these relationships differ in kind. *Pol.* 1259b1 describes the rule of husbands over their wives as being performed πολιτικῶς (cf. line 4).

In 1252a34 Aristotle continues that master and slave nevertheless share common interests. Because of their different capabilities and aptitudes, however, theirs are different duties. The same is true—*mutatis mutandis*—of women (1260a12-14).

According to *Pol.* 1259b, age and the respective degree of maturity, however, can invert the roles of this relationship that are given by nature. The resulting relationship is said to be unnatural (παρὰ φύσιν), but a consequence of the fact that sometimes wives can be more apt to lead a relationship than their husbands (ἡγεμονικώτερον). In addition, in his *Nichomachean Ethics* (1161a1-2), Aristotle mentions that if the wife is wealthier than her husband, she also may rule over him.

Xenophon in his *Oeconomicus* and Plato in book 5 of the *Republic* also talk about the relationship between husbands and wives. Whereas in Plato the traditional family is abolished altogether, both students of Socrates are more willing to entertain the idea that women are admitted into leadership positions; compare, however, *Leg.* 6.781a (women should have public communal meals as well as men) and Aristotle, *Pol.* 1269b14-19, where the dangers are mentioned of letting women be without some sort of rule imposed on them.

Line 2. τὸ δεσποτικόν. The distinction between δεσποτική and πολιτικὴ ἀρχή is made in Aristotle, *Pol.* 1254b4, 1259b1, and 1324a37. The latter is considered to be the more acceptable and friendly; see *Hist. an.* 589a2.

Line 3. θεραπεῦον τὸ τοῦ κρείττονος συμφέρον. The idea that the stronger should not care about the weaker members of society is a very important issue among the Sophists as, for example, reflected in Plato's *Gorgias*.

Lines 3–4. οὐδ' οἷον τὸ τῶν τεχνῶν, μόνου τοῦ ἥττονος ἐπιμελούμενον. The argument that τέχναι properly concern themselves with the welfare of their subjects, which can be regarded as "the weaker," forms an important move in Socrates' refutation of Thrasymachus in *Resp.* 1.340a–342e.

Line 4. ἐξ ἴσου. In *Leg.* 6.777d it is specified that one's behavior in situations in which one is the more powerful and could even abuse this power (as in the case of rule over slaves) really provides one with the opportunity to prove one's character. If one deals with one's weaker opponent as if he were equal (ἐξ ἴσου), that behavior is considered good.

Lines 4–5. τοῦ κοινῇ συμφέροντος. Common interest (τὸ κοινῇ συμφέρον) leads people to form states, according to Aristotle at *Pol.* 1278b23. He makes this statement in a discussion that he himself connects with οἰκονομία and δεσποτεία.

Letter 20: *To an Unknown Recipient, On Ruling*

Once again, the recipient here is not identified, but this may very well be a further extract from the letter to Agrippa that opened this collection. There is in any case nothing very notable about the sentiments expressed here. Presumably the ruler is being exhorted to establish proper rewards for virtuous behavior.

As such, this passage closely resembles Plato, *Leg.* 4.711b, where it is emphasized that the moral leadership of the monarch is of greatest importance for the state. The monarch's example will set a headline for his subjects and thus lead them on the path to virtue (πρὸς ἀρετῆς ἐπιτηδεύματα) or its opposite. Iamblichus's vocabulary in *Letter* 20 has many parallels in Plato's passage; see especially the use of τιμάω and ἀτιμάζω.

Isocrates, too, is convinced that the example set by the ruler inspires his subjects; see *Or.* 2.31, 3.37, and 7.22. Due to the fact that this fragment mainly talks about living an exemplary life, one might suspect that the topics "praise" and "blame," by which a ruler, according to Isocrates

(*Or.* 7.22), may also exert influence over the way his subjects conduct their lives, were discussed before the text of the fragment begins.

Lines 2–3. προτρέπει τε. See Iamblichus, *Protr.* 10,23 Pistelli, where Iamblichus is specifying a mode of protreptic that uses γνῶμαι, including quotations from poetry, to make its point, and exhorts its hearers εἰς πάντα τὰ καλὰ μαθήματά τε καὶ ἐπιτηδεύματα.

Testimonium 1: To an Unknown Recipient, On the Descent of Souls (?)

This testimonium is of special interest for at least two reasons. The first is that it is one of only two references extant to the *Letters* of Iamblichus outside of John of Stobi. While we would not have suspected for a moment that John had invented them, it is good to have some confirmatory evidence of their existence, from a period perhaps a century later than John himself. This passage occurs in a commentary on the *Phaedo* "from the mouth of" (ἀπὸ φωνῆς) Damascius, the last head of the Platonic Academy in Athens before its dissolution by the emperor Justinian in 529 C.E., based on lectures probably delivered at some time in the early decades of the sixth century and compiled from notes taken down by a pupil or pupils. Such documents are inevitably somewhat more garbled and superficial than would have been a formal commentary composed by the man himself, but they are useful nonetheless.

The second aspect of interest resides in the fact that we seem to have reference here to a feature of Iamblichus's doctrine of a rather more technical nature than is evident elsewhere in the *Letters*, not excluding even the *Letter to Macedonius, On Fate*. The topic at issue here, which he obviously dealt with also in his commentary on the *Phaedo* (in connection with the exegesis of the final myth, and in particular, probably, 107e), is the reasons for the descent of souls into embodiment and the question whether all "human" souls (that is, all souls of a level proper to embodiment in humans) must descend, at lesser or greater intervals.

In this introductory portion of the myth, Socrates says:

TESTIMONIUM 1: ON THE DESCENT OF SOULS

Now it is said that when each one has died, the spirit allotted to each in life proceeds to bring that individual to a certain place, where those gathered must submit to judgement, and then journey to Hades with the guide appointed to conduct those in this world to the next; and when they have experienced there the things they must, and stayed there for the time required, another guide conveys them back here during many long cycles of time. (trans. Gallop)

However, there are exceptions, it would seem, to this cyclic movement of souls. Later in the myth, at 113e, we learn that those deemed incurable are hurled into Tartarus, "whence they never more emerge," while at 114c we are told that "those who have been adequately purified by philosophy live bodiless for the whole of time to come, and attain to dwelling places fairer even than those (sc. those bestowed upon "those who are found to have lived exceptionally holy lives," 114b), which it is not easy to reveal, nor is the time sufficient at present."

Now these provisions plainly posed a problem for Platonists who confronted this text with the myth of the *Phaedrus,* where at 248e–249a we seem to be presented with an endless cycle of incarnations, in ten-thousand-year periods, the only special provision being that "those souls who have chosen the philosophical life three times in succession" are exempted from reincarnation for the rest of that particular cycle, while there is no suggestion that any souls are so wicked as to be precluded from reincarnation, even in animal form (though in *Resp.* 10.615e–616a, this would still seem to be the fate of certain notorious tyrants, such as Ardiaeus).

In the face of this, it would seem that Iamblichus propounded a theory that all human souls must be subject to the cycle of rebirth but that we should postulate a set of different conditions for embodiment, depending on the category of soul, of which he distinguishes, broadly, three. He expounds this theory at some length in his *De anima* (§29 Finamore-Dillon):

> In my view, the purposes for which souls descend are different, and that they thereby also cause differences in the manner of the descent. For the soul that descends for the salvation, purification and perfection of this realm is immaculate ($ἄχραντος$) in its descent. The soul, on the other hand, that directs itself about bodies for the exercise and correction of its own character is not entirely free of passions and was not sent away free in itself; while the soul that comes down here for punishment and judgement seems somehow to be dragged and forced.

In his *Commentary on the Phaedo* and, it seems, in a letter, Iamblichus also advanced the theory of different conditions of embodiment and in particular of a class of pure souls who descend voluntarily for the benefit of their fellow-humans and whose descent is free from passions and does not involve separation from the intelligible realm. This begins to sound dangerously like the theory of the undescended soul for which Iamblichus has elsewhere roundly condemned Plotinus (see *In Tim.* frg. 81 Dillon), but in fact Iamblichus is postulating this condition for only a very few *boddhisatvas*, such as, perhaps, Pythagoras, Socrates, and Plato, whereas Plotinus held that each of us retains an element that is "undescended," and that is what Iamblichus objects to.

We can only conjecture to whom Iamblichus would send a letter on such a topic. It would seem more likely to be addressed to a pupil than to a local grandee, but then it would be a fine compliment to such a figure to suggest that he might be one of these special souls!

Lines 4–5. ἀγένητον ... καὶ πρὸς τὰ ἐκεῖ ἀδιάκοπον. The particular force of ἀγένητος here is presumably that of "not involved with generation," but it is a curious use of the word; the embodied soul, however pure, would seem to be inevitably involved in generation. However, the very fact of not relinquishing contact with τὰ ἐκεῖ may be seen as countering the untoward effects of generation, and preserving these souls as "immaculate" (ἄχραντοι).

Lines 5–6. ὡς καὶ αὐτὸς ἐν ἐπιστολαῖς γράφει. This expression clearly indicates that there was a collection of Iamblichus's letters. Obviously, however, we do not have any of these letters Damascius is talking about here.

Testimonium 2

This passage, from *Lecture* 46 of Olympiodorus's *Commentary on the Gorgias* (commenting on 523a1), brings a further welcome confirmation that the collection of *Letters* was known in the Athenian School of the sixth century. A curious aspect of Olympiodorus's discussion, however, is that he speaks as if he was not actually sure of the context of the letter to which he is referring. He loyally rejects the notion that Iamblichus could have been ignorant of the eschatological myth of the *Gorgias*, but he has to resort to a conjecture as to why he might have omitted mention of it. Perhaps, however, the answer to the puzzle is that Iamblichus in the letter did not himself explicitly indicate that he was replying to a request of his correspondent, and Olympiodorus is driven to make this conjecture, on the basis of what he knows to be a feature of other such letters, that they can be framed as responses to specific requests.

This in turn may have some relevance to an issue that we raised in the introduction, as to whether we are perhaps missing a certain amount of introductory matter, of a personal nature, from the corpus of letters that we have, since such matter would not have been germane to the purposes of John of Stobi. We still feel that it is quite probable that there was a certain amount of such introductory matter, but we can conclude that in this case Olympiodorus found no such clue in it—such as, for example, "Since you have asked me to expound to you Plato's meaning in the myths of the *Phaedo* and the *Republic*...."

At any rate, we seem to have here some evidence of an epistolary topic rather different from those presented to us by John, even as was the case with *Testimonium* 1. There the issue concerned the different conditions for the descent of souls; here we seem to be concerned with their fate in the other world. Unfortunately, however, we have no idea what Iamblichus had to say about these myths, though indeed the issue of the descent of souls may well have been raised. In fact, we cannot rule out the possibility that Damascius and Olympiodorus are referring to the same letter.

Line 1. Ἐπεὶ τοίνυν καὶ ταῦτα καλῶς εἴρηται. In what has just preceded, Olympiodorus has made a three-way distinction between the subject matters of the three *nekuiai* (as he calls them), that of the *Phaedo* focusing on the geography of the Otherworld, the *Republic* concentrating on those who are judged, and that of the *Gorgias* on the judges. It is a matter of some interest that he refers to these eschatological myths as *nekuiai*, since the word normally denotes either a funeral ceremony or a magical rite to summon up the dead, but he is presumably influenced by the fact that Odysseus's journey to the Underworld in the *Odyssey* was known as the *Nekuia*. We cannot be sure, however, that Iamblichus would have referred to these myths in the same way, though it is not improbable.

Line 2. τριῶν οὐσῶν νεκυιῶν. These visits to the underworld are to be found in the following passages: *Gorg.* 523a–527e; *Phd.* 107d–115a; *Resp.* 10.614a–616b.

Bibliography

Bergk, Theodor, ed. *Poetae lyrici graeci.* 4th ed. 3 vols. Leipzig: Teubner, 1878–1882.

Ciccolella, Federica. "Stobaios, Ioannes." Pages 563–65 in *Geschichte der antiken Texte: Autoren- und Werklexikon.* Edited by Manfred Landfester. Der Neue Pauly Supplemente 2. Stuttgart: Metzler, 2007.

Czapla, Beate. "Der Kuß des geflügelten Eros: Die Darstellungen des Liebesgottes in Moschos I und Bion Aposp. XIII Gow als hellenistische Kontrafakturen des γλυκύπικρον ἀμάχανον ὄρπετον." Pages 61–82 in *Beyond the Canon.* Edited by Annette Harder, Remco F. Regtuit, and Gerry C. Wakker. Hellenistica Groningana 11. Leuven: Peeters, 2006.

Diels, Hermann, and Walther Kranz, eds. *Die Fragmente der Vorsokratiker: Griechisch und Deutsch.* 7th ed. 3 vols. Berlin: Weidmann, 1954.

Dillon, John M., ed. and trans. *Iamblichi Chalcidensis in Platonis dialogos commentariorum fragmenta.* Philosophia antiqua 23. Leiden: Brill, 1973.

Dillon, John M., and Tania Gergel, eds. *The Greek Sophists.* London: Penguin, 2003.

Dillon, John M., and Jackson Hershbell, eds. *Iamblichus: On the Pythagorean Way of Life.* SBLTT 29. Atlanta: Scholars Press, 1991.

Erler, Michael. *Platon.* Die Philosophie der Antike 2/2; Grundriss der Geschichte der Philosophie. Basel: Schwabe, 2007.

Festa, Nicola, ed. *De communi mathematica scientia liber: Ad fidem codicis Florentini.* Leipzig: Teubner, 1891.

Finamore, John F., and John M. Dillon. *Iamblichus' De Anima: Text, Translation, and Commentary.* Philosophia antiqua 92. Leiden: Brill, 2002.

Gallop, David, trans. *Plato: Phaedo.* Oxford: Clarendon, 1975.

Heil, Günter, and Adolf Martin Ritter, eds. *Corpus Dionysiacum 2: De coelesti hierarchia, De ecclesiastica hierarchia, De mystica theologia, Epistulae*. Patristische Texte und Studien 36. Berlin: de Gruyter, 1991.

Kroll, Wilhelm, ed. *Syriani in metaphysica commentaria*. Commentaria in Aristotelem Graeca 6.1. Berlin: Reimer, 1902.

Mullach, Friedrich Wilhelm August, ed. *Fragmenta philosophorum graecorum*. Scriptorum graecorum bibliotheca. 3 vols. Paris: Didot, 1867–1881.

Norvin, William, ed. *Olympiodori philosophi In Platonis Phaedonem commentaria*. BT. Leipzig: Teubner, 1913. Repr., Hildesheim: Olms, 1968.

Pistelli, Ermenegildo. *Protrepticus: Ad fidem codicis florentini*. BT. Leipzig: Teubner, 1888.

Rabe, Hugo, ed. *Syriani in Hermogenem commentaria*. 2 vols. in 1. BT. Leipzig: Teubner, 1892–93.

Sandbach, Francis H., trans. *Fragments*. Vol. 15 of *Plutarch's Moralia*. LCL. Cambridge: Harvard University Press, 1969.

Saunders, Trevor J., trans. *Plato: The Laws*. Harmondsworth, Eng.: Penguin, 1970.

Smith, Andrew, ed. *Porphyrii philosophi fragmenta*. BT. Stuttgart: Teubner, 1993.

Thesleff, Holger. *The Pythagorean Texts of the Hellenistic Period*. Åbo: Åbo Akademi, 1965.

Wachsmuth, Curt, and Otto Hense, eds. *Ioannis Stobaei anthologium*. 5 vols. in 4. Berlin: Weidmann, 1884–1923. Repr., Berlin: Weidmann, 1958.

Whittaker, John. "The Historical Background of Proclus' Doctrine of the *Authupostata*." Pages 193–237 in *De Jamblique à Proclus: Neuf exposés suivis de discussions*. Entretiens sur l'antiquité classique 21. Geneva: Fondation Hardt, 1975.

Index Rerum

Aristotle (Aristotelian), Iamblichus (Iamblichean), and Plato (Platonic) occur too frequently for inclusion here. Certain literary works are included in this list if they are mentioned rather summarily within the context of our arguments.

Abammon	xiv, 69	Anaximenes	xv
abilities, natural	72	Anebo	xiv
Academy, in Athens	94	Antioch	xix, 80
in the fifth century	xxii	Antiochene	xvi
in the sixth century	xxii	Antiphon	78
dissolution of	94	antiquity, late	70–71
New	xvi	Apamea	xiii, xix, 83, 85
Old	xvi	Apollo	68, 70, 84
accidents	78	of Branchidae	xxiii, 68
accuracy	72	of Delphi	xxiii, 68, 84
acratic acts	62	Apollonius of Tyana	xvi
administration, imperial	xviii, 86	apostles	69
administrator	71	apportionment of fortunes	75
administrators, imperial	xvii, xx, 59	Apuleius	74
adulthood	64	Aramaic	xiii
Aedesius	xiii, xiv, xviii, 72	archangels	81
Agrippa	xviii, xx, 59, 93	Archytas	xv, 59
Alcidamas	60	Ardiaeus	95
Alcinous	74	Aretaeus	88
Alexander of Aphrodisias	60	Arete	xviii, xx, xxiii, 62, 87
allegorization	xxiii, 63	Aristides	60
allusion	64	aristocracy, local	xviii, xx, 59, 62
literary	xxiii	arrow	xxiii, 70
mythological	xxiii	Asclepiades	xvi
ambiguity	xix, xxiii	Asclepius	66
Anatolian	xviii	Asia Minor	59, 70
Anatolius	xiii, xviii, xix, 61, 87	Asphalius	xix, xx, 67, 87

Athenian	69, 78	Chalcis-ad-Belum	xiii
Athenian Stranger (in Plato's *Laws*)	73, 85	chance	75
		character	72, 93
Athenians	79	child	92
Athens	78	children	63
audience, Iamblichus's letters	xxii	Chimaera	xxiii, 63, 64
autonomy, of human soul	82	chords	64
of human will	74	Christian	xvi, 73
of virtuous soul	75	Christian theology	xxii
		Chrysanthius	xiii
bashfulness	90	Chrysippus	74, 81
Basil of Caesarea	xvi, 72, 73	church fathers	69
beast, many-headed	64	citizens	60, 71, 92
beauty	xx, 59, 87	city	67, 92
Absolute	64	class	71
Being	74	classes, lower	78
Bellerophon	xxiii, 63, 64, 65	classics, of literature	62
benefaction	70	of philosophy	62
benefactor	86	Cleareta	xv
beneficence, divine	86	Clement of Alexandria	72
private	86	collection of Iamblichus's letters	xxii
public	86	common interest	93
bishops, Christian	xvii	community	71
blame	93	concerns, material	89
body	64, 74	worldly	89
Branchidae	70	concord	xx, 78
Branchos	70	Constantine	xiv
bringing up children	xx, 85	convention	59
business	73	cosmos	63, 65
		administration of	75
Caesarea	xviii, 73	physical	90
Calcidius	74	courage	xix, xx, 72, 80, 81, 87
Calliope	xxiii, 68, 69, 84	"higher"	81
Cappadocia	xviii, 72, 73	"paradigmatic" level of	81
Carneades	xvi	Crates, the Cynic	xxiii, 65
causal, chain	75, 76	creation, of material things	90
principle, immanent	83	unity of	73
principles	74	creator of false imitations	91
sequence	75	cultural activities	71
causes, natural	78	custom	73
supernatural	78		
Cerberus	64	daemon	75, 77, 88

Damascius	94, 96, 97	Emesa	xiii
deception	91	Empire, early	xvi
decision-making	75	late Roman	86
Delphi	xxiii, 68, 70, 84	later Roman	79
demiurge, sublunary	90	enmities	60
democracy, extreme	60	entertainment	71
Democritus	87	epic poetry	69
Demosthenes	66, 67, 86	Epicurus	xv
descent, of souls	74, 94	epistle	xv, xvi, xvii, xix
of souls, voluntary	96	epistolography, philosophical	xv–xvii
desire	62, 66	equal	93
desires, opposite	79	eschatological myths	97
Dexippus	xviii, xix, xxiii, 68, 83, 84	ethics	xvii, xix, xx
dialectic	xix, xxiii, 68, 69, 83, 84	Eunapius	xiii, xxii, xxiii, 61
dialectical	xxiii, 85	Eustathius	xviii, xxii, 72
dialectical reasoning	69, 70	example set by rulers	93
dichotomy between νόμος and φύσις	59	excess	60
		mitigation of	60
Didyma, oracle of Apollo	70		
Dio Cassius	79	fairness	71
Diogenes Laertius	xvi, 81	fate	xxi, xxii, 73, 74, 75, 76, 77, 82, 83, 94
Dionysius the Areopagite	67		
discord	60	unity of	73
discourse, rational	68	father	92
distributions	71	Favorinus	xvi
divination	76	First Cause	85
divine providence	82	Five Thousand	79
divine, the	63, 91	food	66
divinity	67, 78, 90	force	59
supracosmic levels of	83	Form	74, 87
doctrine of divine providence	75	of the Good	87
doctrines	xxii	multiplicity of Forms	xxi
Dyscolius	xviii, xx, 70	Four Hundred	78
		free will	xxi, 74
education	72, 85	freedom, human	82
educator	67	friendship	90
Egypt	73		
Egyptian	69	Galen	60
Egyptians	xiv	genre	xv, xvii
elements	63	god	xxii, 68, 75, 76, 77, 82, 84, 86, 88
elenchus	xix	of Delphi	84
embodiment	94, 95, 96	assimiliation to	67

godlike	xx	hubris	63
assimilation to the	xx	human being	64
demiurgic level of	83	human, the	63
Good	87	humankind	70
good order	65	hunter	91
goodness	72	husband	92
goods	66	hypostases, principal	77
goodwill, civic	xx		
Gorgias	63	iambic verse	xxiii, 65
Gorgon	xxiii, 63, 65	Iamblichus's correspondents	xvii–xix
government, good	71	life	xiii–xiv
purposes of	71	metaphysical system	xvii, 73
governor	71	philosophical system	xxii
gracelessness	86	works	xiii–xiv
Graces	xxii	works, style of	xxii
gratitude	86	Ideas	88
great natures can produce		identity, unchanging	xx
great evils	73	image-maker	90
Greeks	xxiii	immateriality	81
Guardians of the *Republic*	67	immortal, the	64
		incorruptibility	61
habit	73	Indefinite Dyad	xxi, 74
Hades	95	individuals	86
happiness	71	induction	xix
harmony, civic	xx	infrastructure	73
eternal	64	ingratitude	86
Helios	69	institutions	73
Hellenic	xiv	intellect	xx, xxi, 64, 67, 74
Heraclitus	xxiii, 70, 84	cosmic	89
Hermes	xxiii, 68, 69, 84	hypostatis of	67
Herodotus	60, 70	purified	87
Hesiod	69	intellectual activity	xx
Hiero of Syracuse	xv	potency	xx
Himerius	xvi, xviii, 85	intelligence, discursive	xx
Hipparchus	xv	intelligible realm	74, 77, 88, 96
Homer	69	Ionic	70
Homeric	78	irrationality	79
homonymy	xix, xxiii	Isocrates	93
honors, apportionment of	xx		
household	92	jesting, right and wrong kind of	67
head of	92	John of Stobi	xiv, xvi, xvii, xxiv, xxv,
household management	xx, 93	59, 72, 84, 89, 94, 97	

INDEX RERUM

Josephus	79	Lysis	xv
Judea, dynasts of	59		
judges	61	Macedonius	xvii, xviii, xx, xxi, xxii, 73, 78, 79, 82, 83, 94
Julian	xiv, xvi, xviii, 62, 69, 90		
justice	xvii, xix, 61, 71, 80, 87, 88	Macedonius (the younger)	xix
"higher" aspects of	xx	male	92
"civic" aspects of	xx	marriage	xx, 91
Justinian	94	master	92
		material goods	71
king	69	matter	64, 65, 91
know thyself	84	attractiveness of	66
knowledge	xxiii	maturity	92
		Maximus of Ephesus	xiv
Lamprias catalogue	xvi	Melissa	xv
law	59, 60	members of society	92
law-abiding	59	men	67
law-makers	90	Meno	84
laws	73	*Meno* (Plato's)	84
of cause and effect	74	metaphysics	xix, xx, xxi, xxii, 73, 89
Laws (Plato's)	xxiii, 85	Michael Psellus	69
laypeople, educated	xxii	middle class	60
leadership positions	92	middle ground between extremes	60
leadership, moral	93	midwifery	84, 85
legislation	71	Miletus	70
leisure	71	Minister of Education in Magnesia	85
letter	xv	minors	64
philosophic	xvii	moderation	80
Letters, of various authors	xv, xvi	modesty	xxiii, 69
letter-writing	xvi	monarch	93
Libanius	xvi, xviii, xix, 73, 79, 80, 86	moral	xvii
Licinius	xiv, xvi	mortal, the	64
life	66	multiplicity of phenomena	76
conduct of	94	Multiplicity, principle of	xxi, 74
exemplary	93	municipalities	86
philosophical	95	Muses	xxiii, 69, 84
logic	xix	music	72
love	59	Myia	xv
lower orders, voluntary submission of	79	nature	59, 92
Lucian	69	Nature	xxi, 75, 77, 83
Lucilius	xvii	Nausicaa	79
lyre	xxiii, 64, 70	necessity	74

Neoplatonic	xiii, xx, xxii, 87	Philip	xvi
Neoplatonist	xviii	Philo Judaeus	61, 84
Neopythagoreans	xvi	Philolaus	xv
Nicomachus of Gerasa	xiv, xvi	philosophers	69
nonbeing	90	practicing	xvii
Numenius of Apamea	xiii, xvi	public role of	xvii
		philosophy	xix, 68, 84
Odysseus	79, 97	of Iamblichus' letters	xix–xxii
Odyssey	62, 97	introduction to	xxii
oligarchs	72	popular	xvii, 80
oligarchy	72	pursuit of	71
Olympiodorus	96, 97	solace of	xxii
Olympius	xix, xx, 80, 87	Philostratus	69
One	xxi, 74	Phocylides	61
open-handedness	71	Phrygia	xviii, 62
Oppian	76	Phyllis	xv
opponent, weaker	93	physical realm	74
oracle	70	physical world, administration of	xxi
order of the universe	xxi	generation of	xxi
orderliness	62, 63	physics	xx
Otherworld	97	Pindar	60
otherworldliness	89	Piraeus	78
		Platonic	85, 86, 87, 88, 91
pain	71	Platonism	xiv, 71, 73, 74
parents	85	Platonist	xiii, xv, 74, 88
Parmenides (Plato's)	xv	philosophy	xxii
passions	62, 64, 79, 80, 96	Platonists	xvi, 69, 95
moderation of	62, 63	pleasure	66, 71
multifariousness of	63	Plotinian	83, 87, 89
suppression of	62, 63	Plotinus	xiii, xix, xxi, 63, 64, 68, 74,
Paul, Saint	xvii	75, 76, 77, 80, 81, 91, 96	
Pegasuses	65	Plutarch	xvi, 61, 70
Pergamum	xiv, xviii, 72	Poemenius	xix, xxi, xxii, 82
Peripatetics	xv	poetry	94
Perseus	xxiii, 63, 65	hearers of	94
Persia	73	Porphyrian	xx
Persians	71	Porphyry	xiii, xiv, xviii, 61, 62, 63,
Peter, Saint	69	68, 74, 77, 80, 81	
Phaeacians	62	Posidonius	62
Phaedo (Plato's)	xx, 63	practicing of dying	81
philanthropy	59	praise	93
Philemon	66	preservation	66

priestess of Delphi	70	respect toward the elderly	89–90
priests	70	revenue	71
primal Being	xxi, 74	rewards, apportionment of	xx
principle of the universal coherence of causes	76	rhetoric	xxiv
		Rhodope	xv
private advantage	71	Roman rule	71
Proclus	xiv, 78	Rome	xiii
Prometheus	68	rule	71, 78, 92, 93
property	60	ruler	71, 92, 93
prophecies	68, 70	ruling	xx, 59, 70
protreptic	xv		
providence	xxi, xvii, xxi, 74, 75, 77, 82	sage	74
prudence	xix, xx	school	63
Pseudo-Aristotle	81	School, the	xviii, 72
public good	71	School, Athenian, sixth century	96–97
public works, sponsoring of	71	Scylla	64
public, general	xvii	sea	65
purity	xx	sea voyage	74
pursuit	73	seasons	63
Pythagoras	xiv, xv, 90, 96	security	71
Pythagorean	xiv, xvi, 72, 90	self-control	xvii, xix, xx, 62, 63, 64, 66, 87
Pythagorean pseudepigrapha	xv	self-identity	xx, 80, 81
Pythagoreans	xv, 69	self-indulgence	66
Pythagorizing	xiii	self-respect	90
		selfness	81
Quinnesrin	xiii	Seneca	xvi, xvii
		sequence of cause and effect	83
rational discourse, four levels of	84	shamelessness	90
reality, encosmic level of	83	ship	xxiii, 65, 70
higher, intelligible realm of	xxi	Sicily	xiii
realm of generation and destruction	74	simplicity	xx
		Simplicius	xiv
reason	xx, 62, 79	sinless	77
reasoning, dialectical	68	slave	92
rebirth, cycle of	95	snakes	xxiii, 69
Receptacle, precosmic	82	social contract	71
recollection	84	Socrates	xvi, 65, 71, 84, 92, 93, 94, 96
refutation	xix	Socratics	xvi
reincarnation	95	Sopater	xiv, xvi, xvii, xviii, xix, xx, xxi, xxii, xxiii, xxiv, 68, 83, 85, 86, 87, 90, 91
relationship, natural	92		
unnatural	92		
Republic (Plato's)	xx, 61		

Sopater (the younger)	xvi, xviii, 85	willing	59
sophist	90, 91	sublunar, affairs	75
Sophist (Plato's)	90	realm	77
Sophists	92	sublunary life	76
sorcerer	91	Suda	83
soul	xxi, 64, 74, 87	syllogistic	xix
class of pure	96	symmetry	xx, 87
cyclic movement of	95	Synesius	67
descent of	97	Syria	xiii, xviii, 59, 70, 71
embodied	96	Syrian	xviii, xix, 73
fate in the other world	97	Syrianus	xxiv, 67
higher	83		
higher aspect of	74	Tarsus	xviii
highest part of	78	Tartarus	95
human	77, 94	taxation	71
hypercosmic	76	teachers	85
immaculate	96	teaching	84, 85
lower parts of	63, 65, 66	Telauges	xv
mortal element of	63	temperance	59
parts of	62	Theano	xv
passionate part of	63, 64	Themistius	xviii, 62
powers of	62	Themistocles	xxiii
purifier of	90	Theocritus	72
rational	79	Theognis	61
rational part of	67	Theophrastus	xv, 61
three categories of	95	theurgical	xiv
three parts of (Platonic)	62, 63	theurgy	xiv
undescended	89, 96	Theuth	69
undescended level of	83	Thoth	69
speech, gift of wise and persuasive	69	Thrasymachus	78, 93
Speusippus	xvi	Thucydides	78, 79
spiritedness	62	training	72, 85
staff of Hermes	xxiii, 69	transcendent realm	74
stages of education	85	transcendent superiority	xx
state	73, 93	True Being	90
Stobaeus. *See* John of Stobi		true lie	90
Stoic	xxi, 74, 75, 81, 82	truth	xx, 69, 87, 90, 91
Stoics	xvi	tutors	85
Strato	xv	tyranny	60
style of Iamblichus' letters	xxii–xxiv	Tyrants	95
subjects, of a monarch	93		
of rulers	94	Ulpianus	xviii

underworld 97, 98
universe 75, 83
unstintedness 71
unwillingness to be governed 60

violence, internal and external 71
virtue xix, xx, 60, 61, 63, 67, 75, 80, 87, 88, 89, 93
   cathartic/purificatory level of xix, xx
   civic 63
   civic level of xix, xx, 81, 87
   definition of 85
   four canonical xix, 80
   grades of xx
   levels of xvii, 80
   otherworldly concept of 87
   paradigmatic level of 87
   purificatory 62
   purificatory level of 87
virtuous behavior 93

vocabulary of Iamblichus's letters xxii–xxiv
voluntary descent 96

war 80
wealth 60, 72, 92
welfare 71, 93
wife 92
wisdom xix, 67, 70, 80, 87
women 92
wooden walls xxiii, 70
World Soul xxi, 89
world, divine 90
   material 83
   physical 77
   supra-cosmic 90
writing, invention of 69

Xenocrates xvi
Xenophon 61, 62, 66, 79, 86, 92

Index Verborum

In the following index, the first number represents the number of the letter, the second the number of the fragment, and the third the line number within the fragment, e.g., 14.1.6 refers to Letter 14, fragment 1, line 6. Where there is only one fragment of a particular letter, this is still referred to as the first fragment.

ἄβατος	14.1.6	αἴτιον	8.1.2, 8.1.5, 8.1.9, 8.1.12, 8.4.4, 8.5.9
ἀβίαστος	10.2.7		
ἀγαθοειδής	11.1.8, 16.1.3	ἀκήρατος	18.1.2
ἀγαθότης	11.1.7	ἀκμαῖος	10.1.2
ἀγένητος	T1.4	ἀκριβολογέομαι	6.2.3
ἀγέννητος	8.2.1, 16.2.11	ἀκρόασις	13.2.10
ἄγνοια	1.2.11, 8.6.4	ἀκρότης	8.6.8, 16.2.5
ἁγνός	3.2.4	ἀλγηδών	10.2.11
ἄγριος	3.3.4	ἀλήθεια	8.2.10, 14.1.39, 16.2.3, 18.1.1
ἀγωγή	14.1.37, 14.1.40	ἀληθής	13.2.5
ἀδιάφθορος	1.2.13	ἀλλοίωσις	16.2.15
ἄδικος	1.2.12	ἀλόγιστος	3.3.6
ἀήττητος	10.2.7	ἀμβλυώττω	18.1.6
ἀθάνατος	3.2.1, 8.7.2	ἀμέριστος	8.4.5, 16.2.10
ἄθεος	18.1.3	ἀμερίστως	16.2.8
Ἀθήνη	3.4.4	ἀμετάστατος	16.2.3
αἰδώς	17.1.1	ἄμετρος	3.3.5
αἵρεσις	8.6.3	ἄμικτος	16.2.6
αἴσθησις	14.1.8	ἀμφιβολία	5.1.9
αἰσχρός	<14.1.14>, 14.1.16, 14.1.17, 14.1.19, 17.1.2, 17.1.3	ἀναγκαῖος	8.3.3, T1.3
		ἀνάγκη	8.2.7
αἰσχύνη	14.1.18	ἀναίδεια	17.1.2
αἰτία	8.1.6, 8.1.8, 8.5.3, 8.5.4, 8.5.10, 12.1.2, 12.1.3, 14.1.32, 14.1.37, T1.3	ἀναίρεσις	11.1.3
		ἀναμάρτητος	14.1.38
		ἀνάμνησις	13.2.2
		ἀναμφισβητήτως	5.1.11

ἀναφέρω	4.1.13	14.1.37, 16.1.1, 16.1.3, 16.2.2,
ἀνδραγαθία	10.2.7	16.2.7
ἀνδρεία	10.1.1, 10.1.3, 10.2.6	ἁρμονία	3.6.3
ἀνείδεος	18.1.5	ἄρρην	19.1.1
ἀνέλεγκτος	5.1.5, 14.1.39	ἀρχή	1.1.1, 6.2.2, 6.2.10, 8.1.2,
ἀνήμερος	3.3.4	8.1.4, 8.1.6, 8.2.3, 8.4.9, 8.4.10,
ἀνθρώπινος	1.2.13, 2.2.1, 2.2.2, 8.3.3,	8.4.12, 8.5.5, 8.6.1, 12.1.7, 12.1.8,
13.1.19, 16.4.2	13.1.7, 19.1.2, 20.1.2
ἄνθρωπος	1.2.7, 3.3.5, 3.4.5, 4.1.12,	ἄρχων	1.2.9, 6.1.1, 6.1.4
5.1.2, 6.2.2, 8.4.9, 8.6.2, 8.6.3,	ἀρχηγός	4.1.12
8.6.9, 8.7.1, 8.7.7, 13.1.1, 13.1.6,	ἄρχω	1.1.5, 3.1.4, 6.1.4, 14.1.30,
16.2.17, T2.4	19.1.1, 20.1.3
ἄνισος	8.7.6	ἄσκησις	14.1.28
ἀνόητος	3.4.5	ἀσπάζομαι	3.2.2
ἄνοια	18.1.8	ἀστάθμητος	9.1.10
ἀνόμοιος	9.1.7	ἄστατος	9.1.9
ἀνομοιότης	16.2.11	ἀσφάλεια	3.5.3, 5.1.5
ἀντικαταλλάττομαι	6.2.4	ἀσφαλής	3.6.5
ἀνυπέρβλητος	16.2.5	ἀσώματος	8.2.1
ἀνώλεθρος	8.2.2	ἄτακτος	3.3.6, 8.5.2, 8.5.11, 11.1.4,
ἀξία	2.2.1, 8.6.1, 20.1.4	11.1.7
ἀόριστος	8.5.3	ἀτελής	3.3.1, 14.1.33
ἀπαγορεύω	1.2.2	ἀτιμάζω	3.2.1, 3.2.3, 8.6.13
ἁπαλός	14.1.6	ἄτρεπτος	10.1.1, 11.1.6
ἀπαρακάλυπτος	6.2.7	αὐγή	4.1.3
ἀπεικάζω	4.1.15	αὐθαίρετος	8.2.8
ἀπεργάζομαι	4.1.16	αὐθυπόστατος	8.4.19
ἄπλετος	6.1.2	ἄϋλος	8.2.1, 8.4.2
ἁπλότης	16.2.4	αὐστηρός	1.1.3
ἁπλοῦς	16.4.1	αὐτεξούσιος	8.2.4, 11.1.9
ἀποβλέπω	4.1.5	αὐτοκίνητος	8.2.2, 8.4.19
ἀπογέννησις	4.1.4	αὐτόματον	8.5.1
ἀποδοκιμάζω	13.1.24	ἀφειμένος	8.4.11
ἀποκαθαίρω	1.2.10	ἄφετος	8.2.8
ἀπολιθόω	3.4.5	ἄφθαρτος	16.2.11
ἀπολογισμός	14.1.32	ἀφομοιόω	4.1.9, 8.4.3
ἀπόλυτος	8.2.4, 8.4.11, 8.4.20	ἀφομοίωσις	14.1.10
ἀποσῴζω	3.7.2	ἀφορίζω	8.1.14, 8.5.6, 8.6.4
ἄπταιστος	5.1.5	ἀφορμή	3.6.4
ἀρετή	1.2.5, 2.1.1, 3.2.1, 3.5.1,	ἀχαριστία	15.1.1
3.5.4, 3.6.2, 3.6.3, 4.1.1, 4.1.8, 8.6.5,	ἄχραντος	8.4.3
8.6.10, 14.1.2, 14.1.6, 14.1.27,	ἀχώριστος	12.1.2

INDEX VERBORUM 113

ἀχωρίστως	12.1.2	διαλεκτική	5.1.1, 5.1.8, 5.1.13,
			13.1.11, 13.1.15, 13.1.16, 13.2.6,
βάθρον	3.2.4		13.2.11
βασιλεύς	1.2.1	διαλεκτικός	13.1.13
βεβαιότης	14.1.39	διαλεκτικῶς	13.1.15
Βελλεροφόντης	3.3.2	διαμόρφωσις	16.2.2
βιάζομαι	1.2.11	διανέμω	20.1.4
βίος	1.2.7, 2.2.1, 2.2.3, 4.1.13,	διανόησις	9.1.8, 16.1.2
	6.1.2, 8.3.1, 8.3.3, 10.2.7, 13.1.5,	διάνοια	13.2.7, 14.1.33, 14.1.35
	14.1.17	διανομή	2.2.1, 3.1.4, 8.6.1
βλαβερός	2.2.5, 7.1.3	διάπραξις	2.2.5
βλάστη	14.1.1	διαστασιάζω	9.1.7
βοήθεια	15.1.5	διάσκεψις	13.1.20
βούλησις	8.3.4, 11.1.9	διάταξις	4.1.12, 8.4.17, 8.4.23
Βράγχιδαι	5.1.12	διατείνω	1.2.7, 3.6.2, 5.1.4, 8.5.5
		διατριβή	13.2.1
γενεσιουργός	12.1.4	διαφανής	20.1.2
γένεσις	8.4.5, 8.4.22, 11.1.5, 12.1.3,	διαφερόντως	4.1.8
	12.1.5, T1.4	διαφθείρω	7.1.2
γένος	1.2.5	διαφορέω	8.1.11
γιγνώσκω	3.3.2	διδάσκαλος	14.1.9, 14.1.25
γλυκυθυμία	3.5.2	διδάσκω	13.1.15
Γοργώ	3.4.4	διέξοδος	12.1.8
γνώμη	3.4.2, 9.1.6, 14.1.27	διερευνάω	5.1.11
γνῶσις	13.1.21, 14.1.39	διερεύνησις	5.1.8
γράμμα	13.1.23	διισχυρίζομαι	3.6.1
γυμνασία	13.2.9	δικαιοσύνη	[1.2.4], 2.1.3, 2.2.3
γυμνός	6.2.7	διοικέω	6.1.5, 20.1.2
		διοίκησις	1.2.6
δαίμων	<8.5.8>, 8.5.10	διχογνωμονέω	9.1.7
δεδοκιμασμένος	5.1.4	δόγμα	13.1.12
δελεάζω	1.2.12	δόξα	9.1.9, 10.2.3, 13.1.6
Δελφοί	5.1.7	δοξομιμητικός	18.1.2
δεσμός	8.3.3	δόξασμα	13.2.8
δεσποτικός	19.1.2	δόσις	6.1.2, 6.2.4
διάγνωσις	4.1.10	δράκων	5.1.3
διαζωγράφω	4.1.14	δύναμις	1.2.13, 3.1.1, 10.1.1, 13.1.2,
διάθεσις	4.1.3, 8.6.11		14.1.22, 16.2.19, 16.3.3
διαθρυλέω	8.7.7	δύνασθαι (τό)	8.1.3
διακοσμέω	4.1.3, 11.1.3, 16.2.18	δυσχερής	10.2.10
διακόσμησις	12.1.3	δῶρον	8.7.7, 16.2.18
διαλέγεσθαι, τό	13.1.1		

ἐγγίγνομαι	3.6.5	ἐξαλείφω	4.1.14
ἔγκαιρος	4.1.2	ἐξαπατάω	1.2.11, 18.1.9
ἐγκαίρως	14.1.16	ἐξηρημένος	16.2.4, 16.4.2
ἐγκράτεια	3.5.1	ἐξορίζω	3.3.2, 17.1.2
ἔθος	14.1.10	ἕξις	3.5.3, 10.1.2
εἶδος 1.1.4, 1.2.5, 3.4.3, 10.1.3, 10.2.6, 12.1.5, 16.2.7, 18.1.4, T1.4		ἐξουσία	8.3.2
		ἐπαγωγή	5.1.13
εἰδωλοποιία	18.1.2	ἐπανορθόω	11.1.1
εἰκότως	4.1.15	ἐπανόρθωσις	11.1.2, 11.1.6
εἱμαρμένη 8.1.14, 8.2.6, 8.4.6, 8.4.7, 8.4.8, 8.4.17, 11.1.1, 11.1.3, 12.1.1, 12.1.9		ἐπεισοδιώδης	8.5.2
		ἐπήκοος	5.1.8
		ἐπιδείκνυμι	4.1.3
εἱρμός	8.1.9	ἐπιθυμία	3.1.2
εἶναι (τό)	8.2.2	ἐπικαλέω	3.7.3
εἷς 8.1.3, 8.1.6, 8.1.7, 8.1.8, 8.1.9, 8.1.12, 8.1.13		ἐπικαρπία	8.6.5
		ἐπικοινωνέω	8.4.22
ἕκαστος	4.1.13	ἐπικράτεια	1.1.3, 3.3.5, 8.5.5
ἑκουσίως	8.2.9	ἐπιστήμη 5.1.10, 13.1.9, 13.1.22, 13.2.13, 14.1.39	
ἐλάττωσις	11.1.2		
ἔλεγχος	13.2.7	ἐπιστημονικός	14.1.33
ἕλκω	3.3.6	ἐπιστολή	T1.6, T2.3, T2.5
Ἕλληνες	5.1.12	ἐπιστροφή	18.1.1
ἐμμελής	1.1.3	ἐπισυνίστημι	8.1.10
ἐμπαθής	3.3.1	ἐπίταγμα	1.2.6
ἐμπειρία	13.1.4	ἐπιτελέω	8.1.12
ἔμφυτος	13.1.1	ἐπιτήδευμα 2.2.4, 7.1.2, 20.1.3, 20.1.5	
ἕν	8.1.1, 8.1.2	ἐπιτήδευσις	14.1.7
ἐνάντιος 1.2.2, 2.2.6, 4.1.10, 8.6.9, 13.2.7, T1.1		ἐπίφθονος	1.1.1
		ἔργον 2.2.1, 2.2.3, 4.1.10, 5.1.6, 5.1.13, 6.2.2, 13.1.8, 13.2.11, 14.1.9, 14.1.14, 14.1.15, 14.1.27, 16.1.3	
ἐναπομόργνυμι	4.1.15		
ἐναρμόζω	14.1.24		
ἐνέργεια 4.1.7, 8.2.8, 8.4.2, 10.1.2, 15.1.4, 16.1.2, 16.2.18, 16.3.1, 18.1.2			
		Ἑρμῆς	5.1.2
		εὐδαιμονία	8.7.4
ἐνεργέω	8.2.8, 8.4.19, 13.1.20	εὐδαίμων	6.1.4, 16.4.1
ἔνειμι	2.1.2	εὐεξία	14.1.3
ἐνιαυτός	3.7.1	εὐεργεσία	6.2.3, 15.1.6, 15.1.7
ἔννοια	13.1.6	εὐκαιρία	16.1.4
ἐννοέω	3.3.3, 13.1.10	εὐκοσμία	3.1.3
ἔντευξις	13.1.6	εὐκρίνεια	14.1.33
ἔνυλος	12.1.5	εὐλάβεια	14.1.19
ἕνωσις	8.1.10, 8.5.5, 9.1.2	εὐμενῶς	6.2.8

εὐμετρία	16.1.1	θέσις	13.2.10
εὐνομία	1.2.3	θεωρία	13.1.18, 14.1.38
εὐποιΐα	15.1.7	θῆλυς	19.1.1
εὐπρόσιτος	1.1.4	θηριώδης	3.3.4, 3.3.6
εὕρεσις	13.1.7	θνητοειδής	3.2.1, 8.7.3
εὐσθενέω	6.1.5	θυμός	3.1.2, <10.2.4>
εὐσύμβολος	2.2.4		
εὐσυνάλλακτος	2.2.5	Ἰάμβλιχος	Τ1.1, Τ2.2
εὐταξία	3.1.2, 3.4.1, 8.4.3	ἴδιος	4.1.13, 6.1.7, 9.1.3, 9.1.4
εὐτρεπής	2.2.6	ἴσος	6.2.4, 19.1.4

εὐχαριστία 15.1.8
εὐχαρίστως 15.1.6 καθαρός 4.1.5, 8.4.19, 16.1.2, 16.4.1
ἔφορος 8.5.7, 8.5.9 καθαρότης 16.2.5
ἔχω 4.1.6, 4.1.16 κάθαρσις 13.2.7
καθέλκω 3.4.5
ζηλόω 14.1.10 κάθοδος Τ1.3, Τ1.5
ζῆν (τό) 8.2.2 κακός 7.1.1, 7.1.3, 11.1.2
ζωή 6.1.3, 8.2.5, 8.4.21, 8.6.13, Καλλιόπη 5.1.5
    8.7.3, 8.7.4, 8.7.5, 10.1.3, 12.1.4, κάλλος 1.2.3, 1.2.5, 3.6.2, 16.2.3,
    14.1.29, 16.1.1, 16.2.19, 16.4.2,   16.3.2
    Τ1.4 καλός 3.5.3, 3.7.2, 3.7.3, 4.1.6, 4.1.9,
ζῷον 6.1.9, 13.1.18, 14.1.1   8.6.11, 8.7.2, 10.2.8, 11.1.9, 14.1.7,
    14.1.9, 14.1.12, 14.1.14, 14.1.18,
ἡγεμονία 1.1.5   15.1.4, 16.1.3, 20.1.3
ἡγεμών 4.1.1 καλὸς κἀγαθός 8.6.10–11
ἡδονή 3.2.3, 3.4.1, 10.2.2, 14.1.13 κατασκευή 8.4.18, 14.1.29
ἦθος 14.1.11, 17.1.2 κατάστασις 2.2.6, 10.1.5
ἥμερος 2.2.4 κάτειμι Τ1.2
Ἡράκλειτος 5.1.7 κατευθύνω 4.1.11
κατόρθωσις 4.1.11
θαρρέω 3.6.1 κίνδυνος 10.2.9
θάρσος 10.2.2 κίνησις 8.2.3, 8.4.1, 8.4.11, 8.4.14,
θάνατος 10.2.10   12.1.6
θέα 16.2.2 κοινός 1.2.8, 6.1.7, 9.1.3, 9.1.4, 10.2.5,
θεῖος 4.1.13, 8.2.9, 8.3.4, 8.7.3,   13.1.6, 14.1.27, 15.1.4
    [15.1.4], 18.1.4 κοινῇ 19.1.4
Θεμιστοκλῆς 5.1.10 κοινωνία 4.1.7, 9.1.2
θεοειδής 4.1.16 κοινωνικός 2.2.4
θεός 3.4.3, 4.1.7, 5.1.1, 5.1.7, 5.1.12, κοσμιότης 3.3.3, 3.7.3
    8.3.1, 8.5.8, 8.5.9, 11.1.1, 11.1.10, κόσμος 3.5.2, 3.7.3, 6.2.9, 8.4.1,
    13.1.3, 13.1.13, 16.3.3, 16.4.1,   8.4.15, 8.4.23, 12.1.2
    18.1.1, 18.1.2 κρᾶσις 3.6.3

Κράτης	3.4.2	μονοειδῶς	8.1.13
κράτος	8.1.8	μόριον	13.1.10
κρηπίς	3.5.1	Μοῦσα	5.1.4
κρίσις	4.1.10		
κυβερνητικός	4.1.11	νέκυια	T2.2, T2.5
κύριος	8.7.3	νοερός	4.1.2, 8.2.7, 8.4.2, 8.7.1, 8.7.5,
κωλυτικός	2.2.5		10.1.1, 10.1.2, 16.1.3, 16.2.18, 18.1.8
		νόημα	9.1.6
λογικῶς	13.1.12	νοητικός	18.1.4
λογίζομαι	9.1.7, 13.1.8	νοητός	8.2.10, 8.4.3, 16.2.7, 16.3.2
λόγιος	5.1.2	νομοθέτης	14.1.25
λογισμός	9.1.9, 14.1.38	νόμος	1.2.1, 1.2.6, 1.2.8, 1.2.9, 1.2.10,

λόγος   2.1.2, 3.1.3, 4.1.3, 5.1.5, 8.1.5,   1.2.13
    8.4.18, 8.6.12, 10.1.5, 10.2.4,   νουθέτημα   14.1.26
    10.2.5, 12.1.4, 13.1.11, 13.1.13,   νουθετητικός   14.1.21
    13.1.17, 13.1.18, 13.1.21, 13.1.22, νοῦς   4.1.5, 8.3.1, 9.1.2, 10.1.2, 16.1.2,
    13.2.12, 13.2.13, 14.1.11, 14.1.24,   16.2.1, 16.3.1, 18.1.7
    14.1.28, 14.1.30, 15.1.6, 16.1.1,
    16.2.17, 16.2.18, T1.6   οἶκος   3.4.1, 4.1.13, 9.1.3, [9.1.4]

λύπη	10.2.2, 14.1.13	οἰκείωσις	14.1.7
λυσιτελέω	6.1.8	ὄμμα	4.1.2
		ὁμογνωμονέω	19.1.2
μαιεία	13.2.4	ὁμογνωμοσύνη	9.1.5
μακάριος	6.1.6, 8.6.12, 8.7.5	ὅμοιος	9.1.2, 16.4.1
μαντεία	5.1.8	ὁμοιότης	4.1.14
μεγαλοπρέπεια	6.2.1	ὁμολογέομαι	3.6.1
μεγαλοπρεπής	6.1.2	ὁμονοέω	9.1.6
μεγαλοφροσύνη	6.2.1	ὁμόνοια	9.1.1
μεγαλοψυχία	8.6.7	ὁμοφροσύνη	9.1.8
μέγεθος	1.2.3	ὁμωνυμία	5.1.9
μέθοδος	13.1.9, 13.1.14	ὄν	8.1.1, 16.2.5, 18.1.4
μελέτη	13.1.4	ὄντως	18.1.4
Μένων	13.2.3	ὄργανον	6.2.6
μερίς	8.4.15	ὀρθότης	1.2.10
μέρος	6.1.8	ὁρμή	14.1.20
μέσος	8.7.5, 10.2.4	οὐσία	8.2.1, 8.4.5, 8.4.7, 12.1.3,
μεσότης	16.1.3		16.2.16, 16.3.3
μετουσία	16.3.2	ὄφελος	1.2.7
μέτρον	3.4.1, 3.7.3, 4.1.2, 4.1.6		
μισητός	1.1.2	πάθημα	3.4.6
μοῖρα	8.4.16	πάθος	3.3.4, 10.2.1, 10.2.5
μόνιμος	10.1.2, 10.1.5	παιδαγωγός	14.1.8

παιδεία	14.1.5, [14.1.40]	πρᾶος	1.1.4
παῖς	14.1.3, 14.1.10, 14.1.40	προαίρεσις	8.6.3, 10.2.6
πᾶν	8.4.10, 8.4.11, 8.4.12, 8.4.13,	προγυμνασία	13.1.8
	8.4.14, 8.5.2, 11.1.1	προηγέομαι	4.1.4
πάνδεινος	15.1.5	προηγούμενος	8.1.11, 8.4.4, 8.4.6,
παράγγελμα	14.1.26		16.1.4
παραγωγή	1.2.11	προκαταβάλλω	14.1.6
παράδειγμα	4.1.6, 4.1.13, 14.1.9	πρόκριτος	5.1.4
παραδέχομαι	4.1.4	πρόνοια	8.4.6, 8.4.7, 11.1.8
παρακατατίθεμαι	14.1.34	προοδηγέω	14.1.5
παραμυθία	11.1.2	πρόοδος	14.1.3, 16.2.12
παραπέτασμα	6.2.7	προσδιαλέγομαι	13.2.8
πάρειμι	4.1.10	προσήκω	3.1.3, 4.1.10
παρισόω	1.2.3	προσηλόω	3.2.3
παρουσία	16.2.13	πρόσταγμα	14.1.21
πεπρωμένη	8.4.2, 11.1.5	προστάττω	1.2.2
περιεκτικός	8.1.8	προσηνής	1.1.4
περίοδος	T1.3	πρόσφορος	2.2.3, 14.1.2
περιοράω	8.6.13	πρόσχημα	18.1.7
περιφορά	8.4.2	προτείνω	6.2.8
Περσεύς	3.4.3	προτεταγμένος	8.1.12
πίθος	6.2.5	προτιμάω	8.6.12
πλάστιγξ	6.2.4	προϋπάρχω	8.1.4
Πλάτων	3.2.4, 3.5.3, 18.1.3	πρόφασις	1.2.12
πλῆθος	8.1.6, 8.1.10, 8.4.5	προχέω	6.2.5
πλημμέλεια	11.1.8	πρῶτα (τά)	8.5.5
πλησιάζω	3.4.2	Πυθώ	13.1.23
πλησμονή	3.4.6		
ποιητής	6.2.6	ῥαστώνη	6.1.3
ποίησις	12.1.7	ῥέπω	7.1.3, 8.4.21
πολέμιος	9.1.10	ῥώμη	10.1.4
Πολιτεία	T2.4		
πόλις	1.2.6, 3.4.2, 4.1.12, 6.1.9, 9.1.3,	σεμνός	1.1.3, 13.1.23
	20.1.4	σκοτεινός	18.1.3
πολιτικός	19.1.4	σπέρμα	14.1.5
πολλοί (οἱ)	1.1.1, 8.6.4, 17.1.3, 18.1.7	σπουδαῖος	6.1.4, 8.6.6, 14.1.11, 16.1.3
πολυειδής	3.1.5, 8.1.5	σπουδή	3.2.2
πολυμέριστος	8.1.5, 10.2.6	στέφανος	6.2.9
πόνος	10.2.9	στοιχεῖον	3.7.1, 8.4.15
πρᾶγμα	1.2.4, 13.1.21	συγγένεια	9.1.4
πρακτέος	14.1.29	σύγκρασις	3.7.2
πρᾶξις	8.4.12, 10.2.7	συγκρούω	13.2.8

συγχωρέω	1.2.12	τἀγαθόν	15.1.2
σύλλογος	9.1.3	τάξις	3.1.3, 4.1.2, 8.1.13, 8.1.14,
συμβεβηκός	8.5.4		8.4.3, 8.5.1, 8.5.4, 8.5.6
συμμετρία	3.1.2, 3.6.3, 14.1.24, 16.2.3	ταυτότης	10.1.2, 16.2.3
σύμμετρος	10.2.3	τέλειος	4.1.5, 8.4.20, 8.7.4, 16.3.1,
συμμέτρως	4.1.15, 14.1.15		16.4.1
συμπεφορημένος	8.1.9	τελειότης	8.6.8, 8.6.12, 14.1.4,
συμπλέκω	8.1.7		14.1.38, 16.1.1, 16.2.4
συμπλοκή	8.1.3, 8.1.10, 8.1.12, 8.4.22	τελειόω	4.1.6
συμφέρω	4.1.9, 16.2.14	τέλεος	3.3.1
συμφέρον	6.1.7, 19.1.3, 19.1.5	τελεόω	18.1.5
συμφωνία	3.7.2, 8.4.10, 14.1.13	τελέως	14.1.33, T1.1
συναγωγή	2.1.1, 9.1.1	τέλος	2.1.1, 6.1.4, 8.7.2, 12.1.7,
συναγωγός	8.5.7		12.1.8, 14.1.2, 14.1.36, 14.1.40,
συναγωνίζομαι	3.3.3		16.1.4
συναναφέρω	8.1.4	τεταγμένως	12.1.6, 14.1.4
συνάπτω	8.4.6	τέχνη	13.1.4, 13.1.7, 19.1.3
συναρμόζω	3.6.2	τίμιος	13.1.23
συναρτάω	8.4.4	τιμή	2.2.1
συναυξάνομαι	16.2.14	τύχη	8.5.1, 8.5.6, 8.6.6, 8.7.6., 8.7.7
συναύζω	8.6.10		
σύνδεσις	8.1.7, 12.1.8	ὕλη	3.4.5, 12.1.5
σύνδεσμος	8.1.8	ὑπερβάλλω	1.2.4
συνδέω	8.1.13	ὑπέρογκος	1.1.2
συνέχεια	8.5.4	ὑπεροχή	1.1.1, 16.2.4
συνεχής	6.2.8	ὑποθήκη	14.1.28
συνήθεια	14.1.12	ὑπόστασις	16.2.16
σύνθημα	5.1.3		
συνίσταμαι	4.1.8	Φαίδων	T2.3
σύντονος	14.1.20	φενακισμός	1.2.11
συντυχία	8.6.7	φιλανθρωπία	1.1.3
σύστασις	3.7.1	φιλέω	1.1.5
σχῆμα	19.1.2	φιλία	15.1.6
Σωκράτης	3.5.1, 13.2.2	φιλοσοφία	5.1.4, 13.1.9, 13.1.11,
σῶμα	3.2.3, 8.4.22		13.2.1
σωματοειδής	12.1.4, 16.2.1	φιλόσοφος	T2.6
σωτήρ	1.2.12	φιλοτιμία	14.1.18
σωτηρία	3.6.5, 5.1.12, 6.1.3	φόβος	10.2.2
σωφροσύνη	3.1.4, 3.2.2, 3.3.1, 3.4.4,	φορά	8.2.6
3.5.2, 3.6.2		φρόνησις	4.1.1, 4.1.16
σώφρων	3.7.2	φύλαξ	1.2.13
		φῦλον	3.3.4

φυσικός	13.1.12	χρηστότης	1.1.2
φύσις 6.1.9, 7.1.1, 8.1.5, 8.2.3, 8.2.7,		χρηστῶς	6.2.8
8.4.11, 8.4.13, 8.5.10, 8.6.7, 8.6.8,		χώρα	15.1.3
9.1.4, 11.1.4, 12.1.1, 12.1.6, 12.1.7,		χωριστός	16.3.1
13.1.19, 14.1.3		χωριστῶς	12.1.3
φυτόν	14.1.1		
φῶς	5.1.10, 13.2.5	ψευδής	13.2.5
		ψυχή 3.1.1, 3.2.3, 8.2.1, 8.3.2,	
χαρίεις	6.2.9, 16.1.4	8.4.20, 8.6.8, 8.7.1, 11.1.9, 14.1.6,	
χάρις	6.2.5, 6.2.9	14.1.12, 16.1.1, 16.2.19, 17.1.3	
Χιμαίρα	3.3.3		
χορηγία	6.1.2	ὥρα	3.7.1
χράομαι	4.1.1	ὁρίζω	3.4.1
χρησμός	5.1.9	ὠφέλιμος	2.2.5, 5.1.15
χρηστός	17.1.1		

CPSIA information can be obtained
at www.ICGtesting.com
Printed in the USA
FSOW01n2027220517
34562FS